Dr Michael M. Gruneberg
of the Gruneberg Linkwo
widely acknowledged as a
memory improvement. A
Psychology at University
published a large number
journals, as well as a numb
on the application of memory research. He has also lectured widely in both the UK and the USA and addressed several international scientific conferences. In 1988 he provided the original script for and appeared in *The Magic of Memory*, a programme in the BBC television QED series which illustrated many memory techniques, including his own Linkword Method.

Dr Gabriel C. Jacobs co-writer of the Linkword Portuguese Course BA, PhD, is a Lecturer in Romance Studies at the University College of Swansea. He has been involved for some time in the practical application of language and has published widely on the subject. He is editor of the *International Journal Interactive Multi Media*.

The Linkword Courses have grown out of a large body of published scientific research showing that the imagery method they employ is highly effective in improving the memory for foreign language vocabulary. One study has shown that using this method increases retention from 28% to 88% for a list of 60 Spanish words. Dr Gruneberg has taken this work considerably further, working with linguists and setting out images and testing patterns to create a fully-integrated language-learning system capable of teaching both vocabulary and grammar.

Since it was first published in 1987, the Linkword system has been both highly successful and widely acclaimed.

Language Consultant
Teresa Guerreiro

Also by Dr Michael Gruneberg

LINKWORD
LANGUAGE SYSTEM

PORTUGUESE

Dr Michael M. Gruneberg
and Dr Gabriel C. Jacobs

Language Consultant
Teresa Guerreiro

CORGI BOOKS

LINKWORD LANGUAGE SYSTEM – PORTUGUESE

A CORGI BOOK 0 552 13906 8

First publication in Great Britain

PRINTING HISTORY
Corgi edition published 1992

This book is set in 9/10pt Century
by Colset Private Limited, Singapore.

Corgi Books are published by Transworld Publishers Ltd., 61–63 Uxbridge Road, Ealing, London W5 5SA, in Australia by Transworld Publishers (Australia) Pty. Ltd., 15–23 Helles Avenue, Moorebank, NSW 2170, and in New Zealand by Transworld Publishers (N.Z.) Ltd., Cnr. Moselle and Waipareira Avenues, Henderson, Auckland.

Printed and bound in Great Britain by Cox & Wyman Ltd., Reading, Berks.

Contents

A Foreword by Paul Daniels

As you may know I, Paul Daniels, am a professional magician, and as such am involved in the business of deception. I am also writing this foreword without ever having seen the full text of this book.

Add these two facts together and you may well wonder why or how I can speak with any degree of authority or expect to be believed when I extol the virtues of the Linkword system.

Well, the simple truth is that one Monday morning at nine a.m. I did not speak a single word of Spanish and by five p.m. on the following Friday I knew hundreds of words of Spanish! I know that is true because I counted them!! Please note the use of the word "knew" in the last sentence . . . it was chosen deliberately . . . I knew the words positively enough to KNOW that when I said them they were the correct words. My brain reeled with the excitement of learning so much so fast. At forty-eight years of age I had finally got to the stage of being able to communicate with people of another language . . . and how they loved me for trying.

A few weeks later, with no more lessons other than my own reading of Spanish newspapers and books I went on stage and performed my act entirely in Spanish, and now I am "all fired up" and anxious to learn more. It's wonderful.

Memory systems go back a long way, and I have read many that have suggested their methods could be applied to language learning, but this system is the first I have come across where someone has actually provided a complete system that is "ready to go". When you first read memory systems that use idiotic association as a memory aid it is very easy to think that the idea itself is stupid, BUT IT WORKS!!!

So, do yourself a favour and don't knock it till you have tried it. Once you have found out for yourself how to use your own imagination fully to really "see" the mental images I am sure that like me you will be wondering why this "game" of learning language is not taught in all our schools.

INTRODUCTION

TEST YOURSELF WITH LINKWORD

Picture each of these images in your mind's eye for about ten seconds. For example, the French for *tablecloth* is *nappe*. Imagine yourself having a nap on a tablecloth, as vividly as you can, for about ten seconds.

The French for TABLECLOTH is NAPPE
Imagine having a *NAP* on a *TABLECLOTH*.

The German for GENTLEMEN is HERREN
Imagine a *HERRING* dangling from the door of a *GENTLE-MEN'S* toilet.

The Italian for FLY is MOSCA.
Imagine *FLIES* invading *MOSCOW*.

The Spanish for SUITCASE is MALETA
Imagine *MY LETTER* in your *SUITCASE*.

The French for HEDGEHOG is HERISSON.
Imagine your *HAIRY SON* looks like a *HEDGEHOG*.

The German for LETTER is BRIEF.
Imagine a *BRIEF LETTER*.

The Italian for DRAWER is CASSETTO.
Imagine you keep *CASSETTES* in a *DRAWER*.

The Spanish for WAITRESS is CAMARERA.
Imagine a *WAITRESS* with a *CAMERA* slung around her neck!

NOW TURN OVER

1

○ What is the English for CAMARERA? _____

○ What is the English for CASSETTO? _____

○ What is the English for BRIEF? _____

○ What is the English for HERISSON? _____

○ What is the English for MALETA? _____

○ What is the English for MOSCA? _____

○ What is the English for HERREN? _____

○ What is the English for NAPPE? _____

TURN BACK FOR THE ANSWERS

Do not expect to get them all correct at the first attempt. However, if you feel you got more right than you normally would have – then this course will suit you!

WHO IS LINKWORD FOR?

The short answer is that Linkword is for anyone and everyone who wants to learn the basics of a language in a hurry. It can be used by children or by adults.

The Linkword Courses have been carefully designed to teach you a basic grammar and words in a simple step-by-step way that anyone can follow. After about 10–12 hours, or even less, you will have a vocabulary of literally hundreds of words and the ability to string these words together to form sentences. The course is ideal, therefore, for the holidaymaker or business person who just wants the basics in a hurry so he or she can be understood, e.g. in the hotel, arriving at the destination, sightseeing, eating out, in emergencies, telling the time and so on.

HOW TO USE LINKWORD

1] You will be presented with images like this:

The Portuguese for GOOSE is GANSO
Imagine GANGS O' geese going round together

What you do is to imagine this picture in your mind's eye as vividly as possible.

2] After you have read the image you should think about it in your mind's eye for about 10 seconds *before* moving on to the next word. If you do not spend enough time thinking about the image it will not stick in your memory as well as it should.

3] After you have been presented with a number of words you will be given a Portuguese word and asked to give the English.

4] After you have translated from Portuguese to English you will be asked to translate from English to Portuguese.

5] When you are asked to translate sentences from English to Portuguese or Portuguese to English you can write the answer in.

6] Sometimes the word in Portuguese and in English is the same or very similar. For example, the Portuguese for "sardine" is "sardinha". When this happens you will be asked to associate the word in some way with Port wine. For example:

Imagine a sardine in a bottle of Port wine.

Whenever port wine comes to mind, therefore, you will know the word is the same or similar in both English and Portuguese.

7] It is very important to realise that some groups of words are more difficult to learn than others. If this happens do not worry, just go on to the next set of words and forget you have had any difficulty. The important thing to appreciate is how much you do learn very quickly. Even if you feel you want to go back, therefore, you are strongly advised to carry on to the end of a section before going back to look at what you have already done.

8] The examples given in the course may well strike you as silly and bizarre. The fact is that they have deliberately been constructed to illustrate parts of grammar and to get away from the idea that you should remember useful phrases "parrot fashion".

9] The pronunciation of each new word presented is given in brackets on the right hand side of the page. Do not worry too much about pronunciations to begin with. The approximate pronunciation given in brackets will allow you to be understood. If you would like to listen to the exact pronunciation, a- audio-tape containing all the words on the course is available from Corgi Books.

10] **ACCENTS**
You will notice that some words have an accent over certain letters like Á. They do affect the pronunciation of certain words, and they may be used to distinguish between certain words which are spelled the same.

However, you should not worry about the pronunciation, as this is done correctly on the audio tape, and the approximate pronunciation you are given will allow you to be understood.

SOME USEFUL HINTS

1. It is usually best to go through the course as quickly as possible. Many people can get through most of the course in a weekend, especially if they start on Friday evening.

2. Take a break of about 10 minutes between each section, and always *stop* if you feel tired.

3. Don't worry about forgetting a few words, and do not go back to relearn words you have forgotten. Just think of how much you are learning, and try to pick up the forgotten words when it comes to revising.

4. Revise after Section 4, Section 8 and at the end of the course. Then revise the whole course a week later and a month later.

5. Don't worry if you forget some of the words or grammar after a time. Relearning is extremely fast, and going through the book for a few hours just before you go abroad will quickly get you back to where you were.

6. The course will not give you conversational fluency. You can't expect this until you go abroad and live in a country for a period of time. What it will give you very rapidly is the ability to survive in a large number of situations you will meet abroad. Once you have got this framework, you will find it much easier to pick up more words and grammar when you travel.

IMPORTANT NOTE

The first section of the course can be basically regarded as a training section designed to get you into the Linkword method quickly and easily.

After about 45 minutes you will have a vocabulary of about 30 words and be able to translate sentences. Once you have finished Section 1 you will have the confidence to go through the rest of the course just as quickly. Animal words are used in the first section as they are a large group of "easy to image" words. Many animal words of course are useful to have as they are often met abroad, e.g. dog, cat, etc., or they are edible!

Finally, when it comes to translating sentences the answers are given at the foot of the page. You may find it useful to cover up the answers before you tackle the translations.

Section 1   ANIMALS AND DESCRIPTIVE WORDS

ANIMALS

THINK OF EACH IMAGE IN YOUR MIND'S EYE FOR ABOUT TEN SECONDS

○ The Portuguese for CAT is GATO   (GATOO)
  Imagine a cat eating a beautiful GATEAU.

○ The Portuguese for DOG is CÃO   (KAONG)
  Imagine a dog chasing a COW.

○ The Portuguese for BULL is TOURO   (TOROO)
  Imagine a TOREAdor fighting a bull.

○ The Portuguese for COW is VACA   (VAKA)
  Imagine a cow with a VACUum cleaner,
  cleaning the field.

○ The Portuguese for DUCK is PATO   (PATOO)
  Imagine duck PATÉ.

○ The Portuguese for SARDINE is
  SARDINHA   (SARDEENYA)
  Imagine SARDINES in Port wine.

○ The Portuguese for OCTOPUS is POLVO   (POLVOO)
  Imagine PULVerising an octopus.

○ The Portuguese for GOOSE is GANSO   (GANSOO)
  Imagine GANGS O' geese going round
  together.

○ The Portuguese for SALMON is SALMÃO   (SALMAONG)
  Imagine SALMON swimming in Port wine.

○ The Portuguese for RABBIT is COELHO   (KOO ELYOO)
  Imagine hearing a rabbit CALL YOU.

YOU CAN WRITE YOUR ANSWERS IN

○ What is the English for COELHO? _____

○ What is the English for SALMÃO? _____

○ What is the English for GANSO? _____

○ What is the English for POLVO? _____

○ What is the English for SARDINHA? _____

○ What is the English for PATO? _____

○ What is the English for VACA? _____

○ What is the English for TOURO? _____

○ What is the English for CÃO? _____

○ What is the English for GATO? _____

TURN BACK FOR THE ANSWERS

COVER UP THE LEFT HAND PAGE BEFORE ANSWERING

○ What is the Portuguese for rabbit? _____

○ What is the Portuguese for salmon? _____

○ What is the Portuguese for goose? _____

○ What is the Portuguese for octopus? _____

○ What is the Portuguese for sardine? _____

○ What is the Portuguese for duck? _____

○ What is the Portuguese for cow? _____

○ What is the Portuguese for bull? _____

○ What is the Portuguese for dog? _____

○ What is the Portuguese for cat? _____

TURN BACK FOR THE ANSWERS

ELEMENTARY GRAMMAR

The first thing to learn about Portuguese words is that all *things* (sometimes called nouns), whether living or non-living, are either MASCULINE or FEMININE.

You could guess that TOURO (bull) is masculine, and VACA (cow) is feminine.

With some words you can't guess. But usually if the word ends in an "O" then it is MASCULINE.

If it ends in an "A" then it is FEMININE.

So, for example:

> PATO (duck) is masculine since it ends in an "O".
>
> SARDINHA (sardine) is feminine since it ends in an "A".

Now cover up the answers below and give the genders of the following:

(You can write your answers in)

PATO   _____

GATO   _____

SARDINHA   _____

SALMÃO   _____

VACA   _____

The answers are:

PATO is MASCULINE

GATO is MASCULINE

SARDINHA is FEMININE

SALMÃO is MASCULINE

VACA is FEMININE

SOME MORE ANIMALS

THINK OF EACH IMAGE IN YOUR MIND'S EYE FOR ABOUT TEN SECONDS

○ BIRD is PÁSSARO   (PASAROO)
Imagine hearing a bird PASS A RUde comment.

○ FISH is PEIXE   (PE ISH)
Imagine you PAY EACH fish some money.

○ FLY is MOSCA   (MOSHKA)
Imagine MOSCOW being invaded by flies.

○ HORSE is CAVALO   (KAVALOO)
Imagine the CAVALRY on horses.

○ INSECT is INSECTO   (EENSETOO)
Imagine INSECTS crawling around a glass of Port wine.

○ JELLYFISH is ALFORRECA   (ALFORREKA)
Imagine that I'LL FORESAKE HER for a jellyfish.

○ MOSQUITO is MOSQUITO   (MOOSHKEETOO)
Imagine MOSQUITOS buzzing around a bottle of Port wine.

○ TURKEY is PERÚ   (PEROO)
Imagine turkeys come from PERU.

○ PRAWN is GAMBA   (GAMBA)
Imagine prawns GAMBOling in the water.

○ LOBSTER is LAGOSTA   (LAGOSHTA)
Imagine the problem with lobsters is that THEY COST A lot.

YOU CAN WRITE YOUR ANSWERS IN

○ What is the English for LAGOSTA? _____

○ What is the English for GAMBA? _____

○ What is the English for PERÚ? _____

○ What is the English for MOSQUITO? _____

○ What is the English for ALFORRECA? _____

○ What is the English for INSECTO? _____

○ What is the English for CAVALO? _____

○ What is the English for MOSCA? _____

○ What is the English for PEIXE? _____

○ What is the English for PÁSSARO? _____

TURN BACK FOR THE ANSWERS

16

COVER UP THE LEFT HAND PAGE BEFORE ANSWERING

○ What is the Portuguese for lobster? _____

○ What is the Portuguese for prawn? _____

○ What is the Portuguese for turkey? _____

○ What is the Portuguese for mosquito? _____

○ What is the Portuguese for jellyfish? _____

○ What is the Portuguese for insect? _____

○ What is the Portuguese for horse? _____

○ What is the Portuguese for fly? _____

○ What is the Portuguese for fish? _____

○ What is the Portuguese for bird? _____

TURN BACK FOR THE ANSWERS

ELEMENTARY GRAMMAR

You have already learned that usually nouns (things) are masculine if they end in an "O" and feminine if they end in an "A".

Some words do not end in either an "O" or an "A", like PEIXE (fish) and PERÚ (turkey).

In such cases you can assume they are masculine – you will be told if they are feminine.

If the word is MASCULINE, then the word for THE in Portuguese is O (pronounced oo), often just like the ending of the word it goes with.

So, for example:

    THE BULL is O TOURO

    THE HORSE is O CAVALO

    THE FISH is O PEIXE

If the word is FEMININE, then the word for THE is A (pronounced like the "u" in "curl"). Again, it is like the ending of the word it goes with.

So, for example,

    THE COW is A VACA

    THE FLY is A MOSCA

    THE PRAWN is A GAMBA

Remember that the word A in Portuguese means THE in the feminine. It doesn't mean "a" in the English sense.

Now cover up the answers below and translate the following:

(You can write your answers in)

1. THE BIRD
2. THE INSECT
3. THE LOBSTER
4. THE JELLYFISH
5. THE OCTOPUS

The answers are:

1. O PÁSSARO
2. O INSECTO
3. A LAGOSTA
4. A ALFORRECA
5. O POLVO

Now cover up the answers below and translate the following:

(You can write your answers in)

1. A SARDINHA
2. O CÃO
3. O MOSQUITO
4. A GAMBA
5. A MOSCA
6. O PEIXE
7. O PERÚ

The answers are:

1. THE SARDINE
2. THE DOG
3. THE MOSQUITO
4. THE PRAWN
5. THE FLY
6. THE FISH
7. THE TURKEY

SOME DESCRIPTIVE WORDS (ADJECTIVES)

THINK OF EACH IMAGE IN YOUR MIND'S EYE FOR ABOUT TEN SECONDS

○ The Portuguese for SMALL is PEQUENO   (PEKENOO)
Imagine wearing a SMALL BIKINI.

○ The Portuguese for TIRED is CANSADO   (KANSADOO)
Imagine thinking, "What CAN SIR DO when he is TIRED?"

○ The Portuguese for QUIET is
TRANQUILO   (TRANKWEELOO)
Imagine being QUIET and TRANQUIL.

○ The Portuguese for CLEAN is LIMPO   (LEEMPOO)
Imagine a man with a very CLEAN face, LIMPING away.

○ The Portuguese for DIRTY is SUJO   (SOOjOO)*
Imagine being dirty SUITS YOU.

*Please note that in the pronunciation guidelines, a small letter j should be pronounced like the "s" in the English word "measure".

YOU CAN WRITE YOUR ANSWERS IN

○ What is the English for SUJO? _____

○ What is the English for LIMPO? _____

○ What is the English for TRANQUILO? _____

○ What is the English for CANSADO? _____

○ What is the English for PEQUENO? _____

TURN BACK FOR THE ANSWERS

22

COVER UP THE LEFT HAND PAGE BEFORE ANSWERING

○ What is the Portuguese for dirty?   _____

○ What is the Portuguese for clean?   _____

○ What is the Portuguese for quiet?   _____

○ What is the Portuguese for tired?   _____

○ What is the Portuguese for small?   _____

TURN BACK FOR THE ANSWERS

ELEMENTARY GRAMMAR

The Portuguese for IS is ESTÁ (pronounced ESHTA).

Imagine A STAR IS born.

So, to say THE DUCK IS you simply say O PATO ESTÁ.

THE COW IS is A VACA ESTÁ.

To say THE DUCK IS TIRED you simply say:

O PATO ESTÁ CANSADO

To say THE BULL IS TIRED you simply say:

O TOURO ESTÁ CANSADO

If the noun is feminine, like A VACA (the cow), then the ending of the adjective changes to 'A'.

So,

THE COW IS TIRED is A VACA ESTÁ CANSADA
(not CANSADO)

THE JELLYFISH IS QUIET is A ALFORRECA ESTÁ
TRANQUILA

Often, in little sentences like THE BULL IS TIRED or THE COW IS QUIET, all you need to do is to make sure that the ending of the adjective ("tired", "quiet", etc.) is the same as the word for "the" – either "O" or "A".

For example,

A VACA ESTÁ TRANQUILA
O TOURO ESTÁ TRANQUILO

Now cover up the answers below and translate the following:

(You can write your answers in)

1. O PEIXE ESTÁ SUJO
2. O PÁSSARO ESTÁ CANSADO
3. O PERÚ ESTÁ LIMPO
4. O COELHO ESTÁ TRANQUILO
5. A LAGOSTA ESTÁ CANSADA

The answers are:

1. THE FISH IS DIRTY
2. THE BIRD IS TIRED
3. THE TURKEY IS CLEAN
4. THE RABBIT IS QUIET
5. THE LOBSTER IS TIRED

Now cover up the answers below and translate the following:

(You can write your answers in)

1. THE SARDINE IS QUIET
2. THE COW IS TIRED
3. THE BULL IS CLEAN
4. THE DOG IS QUIET
5. THE HORSE IS TIRED

The answers are:

1. A SARDINHA ESTÁ TRANQUILA
2. A VACA ESTÁ CANSADA
3. O TOURO ESTÁ LIMPO
4. O CAÕ ESTÁ TRANQUILO
5. O CAVALO ESTÁ CANSADO

ELEMENTARY GRAMMAR

When a noun and an adjective come together, like CLEAN INSECT or QUIET COW, then in Portuguese the adjective usually comes AFTER the noun.

So,

      THE CLEAN OCTOPUS is O POLVO LIMPO

            THE QUIET FLY is A MOSCA TRANQUILA

        THE TIRED INSECT is O INSECTO CANSADO

Now cover up the answers below and translate the following:

(You can write your answers in)

1. A GAMBA PEQUENA ESTÁ SUJA
2. O PATO TRANQUILO ESTÁ CANSADO
3. O GATO LIMPO ESTÁ TRANQUILO
4. O SALMÃO CANSADO ESTÁ TRANQUILO
5. A ALFORRECA TRANQUILA ESTÁ SUJA

The answers are:

1. THE SMALL PRAWN IS DIRTY
2. THE QUIET DUCK IS TIRED
3. THE CLEAN CAT IS QUIET
4. THE TIRED SALMON IS QUIET
5. THE QUIET JELLYFISH IS DIRTY

Now cover up the answers below and translate the following:

(You can write your answers in)

1. THE SMALL INSECT IS QUIET
2. THE TIRED OCTOPUS IS CLEAN
3. THE SMALL BIRD IS TIRED
4. THE QUIET FLY IS TIRED
5. THE SMALL GOOSE IS DIRTY

The answers are:

1. O INSECTO PEQUENO ESTÁ TRANQUILO
2. O POLVO CANSADO ESTÁ LIMPO
3. O PÁSSARO PEQUENO ESTÁ CANSADO
4. A MOSCA TRANQUILA ESTÁ CANSADA
5. O GANSO PEQUENO ESTÁ SUJO

IMPORTANT NOTE
Some of the sentences in this course might strike you as being a bit odd!

However, they have been carefully constructed to make you think much more about what you are translating. This helps the memory process and gets away from the idea of learning useful phrases "parrot fashion".

But of course, having learned with the help of these seemingly odd sentences you can easily construct your own sentences to suit your particular needs.

Section 2 HOTEL/HOME, FURNITURE, COLOURS

FURNITURE AND FITTINGS

THINK OF EACH IMAGE IN YOUR MIND'S EYE FOR ABOUT TEN SECONDS

○ The Portuguese for BED is CAMA   (KAMA)
Imagine a CAMEL lying on your bed.

○ The Portuguese for TABLE is MESA   (MEZA)
Imagine a MAZE O' tables – and you get lost.

○ The Portuguese for DRAWER is GAVETA   (GAVETA)
Imagine someone had a drawer and GAVE IT Away.

○ The Portuguese for CHAIR is CADEIRA   (KADE IRA)
Imagine I COULD HEAR HER sitting on a chair.

○ The Portuguese for CUPBOARD is
ARMÁRIO   (ARMARYOO)
Imagine you keep a large ARMOURY in your cupboard.

○ The Portuguese for CLOCK is RELÓGIO   (ReLOjYOO)*
Imagine a funny clock that RELOADS YOU when you wind it up.

○ The Portuguese for CURTAIN is CORTINA   (KOORTEENA)
Imagine you CONCERTINA a curtain when you close it.

○ The Portuguese for CUSHION is
ALMOFADA   (ALMOOFADA)
Imagine thinking, "I'LL MOVE FATHER off the cushion."

○ The Portuguese for MIRROR is ESPELHO   (ESHPELYOO)
Imagine they EXPEL YOU from school for breaking mirrors.

○ The Portuguese for WARDROBE is
GUARDA-ROUPA (m)   (GWARDA ROOPA)
Imagine you GUARD A ROPE in your wardrobe.

*Please note that in the pronunciation guidelines, a small letter e should be pronounced like the "u" in the English word "curl". Remember too that a small letter j is pronounced like the "s" in "measure".

31

YOU CAN WRITE YOUR ANSWERS IN

○ What is the English for GUARDA-ROUPA (m)? _____

○ What is the English for ESPELHO? _____

○ What is the English for ALMOFADA? _____

○ What is the English for CORTINA? _____

○ What is the English for RELÓGIO? _____

○ What is the English for ARMÁRIO? _____

○ What is the English for CADEIRA? _____

○ What is the English for GAVETA? _____

○ What is the English for MESA? _____

○ What is the English for CAMA? _____

TURN BACK FOR THE ANSWERS

COVER UP THE LEFT HAND PAGE BEFORE ANSWERING

○ What is the Portuguese for wardrobe? _____

○ What is the Portuguese for mirror? _____

○ What is the Portuguese for cushion? _____

○ What is the Portuguese for curtain? _____

○ What is the Portuguese for clock? _____

○ What is the Portuguese for cupboard? _____

○ What is the Portuguese for chair? _____

○ What is the Portuguese for drawer? _____

○ What is the Portuguese for table? _____

○ What is the Portuguese for bed? _____

TURN BACK FOR THE ANSWERS

COLOURS

**THINK OF EACH IMAGE IN YOUR MIND'S EYE FOR
ABOUT TEN SECONDS**

○ The Portuguese for BLACK is PRETO   (PRETOO)
Imagine a PRETTY BLACK ROSE.

○ The Portuguese for WHITE is BRANCO   (BRANKOO)
Imagine a BROWN COW painted WHITE.

○ The Portuguese for YELLOW is AMARELO (AMARELOO)
Imagine a YELLOW ARMADILLO.

○ The Portuguese for RED is VERMELHO   (VERMELYOO)
Imagine a deep RED VERMILION colour.

○ The Portuguese for BLUE is AZUL   (AZOOL)
Imagine that A ZOO'LL pay anything for a
BLUE tiger.

○ The Portuguese for GREEN is VERDE   (VERD)
Imagine the composer VERDI dressed in a
GREEN suit.

○ The Portuguese for BROWN is
CASTANHO   (KASHTANYOO)
Imagine saying, "I CAN'T STAND YOU in
your BROWN socks."

YOU CAN WRITE YOUR ANSWERS IN

○ What is the English for CASTANHO? _____

○ What is the English for VERDE? _____

○ What is the English for AZUL? _____

○ What is the English for VERMELHO? _____

○ What is the English for AMARELO? _____

○ What is the English for BRANCO? _____

○ What is the English for PRETO? _____

TURN BACK FOR THE ANSWERS

COVER UP THE LEFT HAND PAGE BEFORE ANSWERING

O What is the Portuguese for brown?   _____

O What is the Portuguese for green?   _____

O What is the Portuguese for blue?   _____

O What is the Portuguese for red?   _____

O What is the Portuguese for yellow?   _____

O What is the Portuguese for white?   _____

O What is the Portuguese for black?*   _____

TURN BACK FOR THE ANSWERS

*Another word for BLACK is NEGRO.

SOME ADJECTIVES TO HELP MAKE SENTENCES

THINK OF EACH IMAGE IN YOUR MIND'S EYE FOR ABOUT TEN SECONDS

○ The Portuguese for FREE is LIVRE   (LEEVR)
  Imagine being FREE to LEAVE HER.

○ The Portuguese for OLD is VELHO   (VELYOO)
  Imagine a German asking, "VILL YOU be
  OLD one day?"

○ The Portuguese for UGLY is FEIO   (FE YOO)
  Imagine a FEW UGLY people.

YOU CAN WRITE YOUR ANSWERS IN

○ What is the English for FEIO? _____

○ What is the English for VELHO? _____

○ What is the English for LIVRE? _____

TURN BACK FOR THE ANSWERS

COVER UP THE LEFT HAND PAGE BEFORE ANSWERING

○ What is the Portuguese for ugly? _____

○ What is the Portuguese for old? _____

○ What is the Portuguese for free? _____

TURN BACK FOR THE ANSWERS

ELEMENTARY GRAMMAR

You may remember from Section 1 that the ending of an adjective changes with the gender of the noun.

So,

THE TIRED BULL is O TOURO CANSAD<u>O</u>

THE TIRED COW is A VACA CANSAD<u>A</u>

You may have noticed, however, that you have just been given some adjectives which do not end in either O or A: like LIVRE (free) and AZUL (blue).

When this is the case, do not make any change to the adjective – whatever it goes with.

For example,

THE BULL IS FREE is O TOURO ESTÁ LIVRE

THE COW IS FREE is A VACA ESTÁ LIVRE

Now cover up the answers below and translate the following:

(You can write your answers in)

1. A GAVETA VELHA ESTÁ FEIA
2. A MESA BRANCA ESTÁ LIVRE
3. A CAMA PRETA ESTÁ CANSADA
4. O ESPELHO AZUL ESTÁ LIVRE
5. A CORTINA FEIA ESTÁ VELHA

The answers are:

1. THE OLD DRAWER IS UGLY
2. THE WHITE TABLE IS FREE
3. THE BLACK BED IS TIRED
4. THE BLUE MIRROR IS FREE
5. THE UGLY CURTAIN IS OLD

Now cover up the answers below and translate the following:

(You can write your answers in)

1. THE BROWN CUPBOARD IS TIRED
2. THE BLUE WARDROBE IS FREE
3. THE YELLOW CHAIR IS FREE
4. THE GREEN FLY IS FREE
5. THE OLD CLOCK IS TIRED

The answers are:

1. O ARMÁRIO CASTANHO ESTÁ CANSADO
2. O GUARDA-ROUPA AZUL ESTÁ LIVRE
3. A CADEIRA AMARELA ESTÁ LIVRE
4. A MOSCA VERDE ESTÁ LIVRE
5. O RELÓGIO VELHO ESTÁ CANSADO

MORE FURNITURE AND FITTINGS

THINK OF EACH IMAGE IN YOUR MIND'S EYE FOR ABOUT TEN SECONDS

○ The Portuguese for BLANKET is MANTA (MANTA)
Imagine asking a MAN TO give you a blanket.

○ The Portuguese for MATTRESS is
COLCHÃO (KOLSHAONG)
Imagine lumps of COAL SHOW through your
mattress.

○ The Portuguese for COMB is PENTE (PENT)
Imagine a comb BENT double.

○ The Portuguese for BRUSH is ESCOVA (ESHKOVA)
Imagine the house IS COVERED with
brushes.

○ The Portuguese for FLOOR is CHÃO (SHAONG)
Imagine you are SHOWN the floor.

○ The Portuguese for WALL is PAREDE (f) (PARED)
Imagine watching a PARADE from a high
wall.

○ The Portuguese for ROOF is TECTO (TETOO)
Imagine a TATOO on a roof.

○ The Portuguese for DOOR is PORTA (PORTA)
Imagine an hotel PORTER opening a door.

○ The Portuguese for WINDOW is JANELA (jANELA)*
Imagine spraying a window with CHANEL
No. 5 perfume.

○ The Portuguese for RUG is TAPETE (TAPET)
Imagine you take your pipe and TAP IT on a
rug.

*Remember that the small j is pronounced like the "s" in "measure".

45

YOU CAN WRITE YOUR ANSWERS IN

○ What is the English for TAPETE? _____

○ What is the English for JANELA? _____

○ What is the English for PORTA? _____

○ What is the English for TECTO? _____

○ What is the English for PAREDE (f)? _____

○ What is the English for CHÃO? _____

○ What is the English for ESCOVA? _____

○ What is the English for PENTE? _____

○ What is the English for COLCHÃO? _____

○ What is the English for MANTA? _____

TURN BACK FOR THE ANSWERS

COVER UP THE LEFT HAND PAGE BEFORE ANSWERING

O What is the Portuguese for rug?   _____

O What is the Portuguese for window?   _____

O What is the Portuguese for door?   _____

O What is the Portuguese for roof?   _____

O What is the Portuguese for wall?   _____

O What is the Portuguese for floor?   _____

O What is the Portuguese for brush?   _____

O What is the Portuguese for comb?   _____

O What is the Portuguese for mattress?   _____

O What is the Portuguese for blanket?   _____

TURN BACK FOR THE ANSWERS

MORE FURNITURE AND FITTINGS

THINK OF EACH IMAGE IN YOUR MIND'S EYE FOR ABOUT TEN SECONDS

○ The Portuguese for KITCHEN is COZINHA (KOOZEENYA)
Imagine being COSY IN A kitchen.

○ The Portuguese for BALCONY is VARANDA (VARANDA)
Imagine your balcony is like an ornate VERANDAH.

○ The Portuguese for ROOM is QUARTO (KWARTOO)
Imagine rooms divided into QUARTERS.

○ The Portuguese for HOUSE is CASA (KAZA)
Imagine owning a house in CASAblanca.

○ The Portuguese for TAP is TORNEIRA (TOORNEIRA)
Imagine you get a TORN EAR After catching it on a tap.

○ The Portuguese for BATH is BANHO (BANYOO)
Imagine they BAN YOU from taking a bath.

○ The Portuguese for TOILET is RETRETE (f) (RETRET)
Imagine RETREATING to the toilet.

○ The Portuguese for SHOWER is DUCHE (DOOSH)
Imagine asking, "DO SHE shower this morning?"

○ The Portuguese for WASHBASIN is LAVATÓRIO (LAVATORYOO)
Imagine using a washbasin as a LAVATORY.

○ The Portuguese for SHELF is PRATELEIRA (PRATELEIRA)
Imagine little children PRATTLE HERE on a shelf.

YOU CAN WRITE YOUR ANSWERS IN

○ What is the English for PRATELEIRA? _____

○ What is the English for LAVATÓRIO? _____

○ What is the English for DUCHE? _____

○ What is the English for RETRETE (f)? _____

○ What is the English for BANHO? _____

○ What is the English for TORNEIRA? _____

○ What is the English for CASA? _____

○ What is the English for QUARTO? _____

○ What is the English for VARANDA? _____

○ What is the English for COZINHA? _____

TURN BACK FOR THE ANSWERS

COVER UP THE LEFT HAND PAGE BEFORE ANSWERING

○ What is the Portuguese for shelf? _____

○ What is the Portuguese for washbasin? _____

○ What is the Portuguese for shower? _____

○ What is the Portuguese for toilet? _____

○ What is the Portuguese for bath? _____

○ What is the Portuguese for tap? _____

○ What is the Portuguese for house? _____

○ What is the Portuguese for room? _____

○ What is the Portuguese for balcony? _____

○ What is the Portuguese for kitchen? _____

TURN BACK FOR THE ANSWERS

FOUR VERBS

THINK OF EACH IMAGE IN YOUR MIND'S EYE FOR ABOUT TEN SECONDS

○ The Portuguese for HAS is TEM   (TENG)
  Imagine he HAS the TIME.

○ The Portuguese for WANTS is QUER   (KER)
  Imagine thinking, "I don't CARE what he
  WANTS."

○ The Portuguese for EATS is COME   (KOM)
  Imagine saying, "He EATS his COMB."

○ The Portuguese for SEES is VÊ   (VE)
  Imagine a German asking, "Vich VAY do I
  SEE?"

YOU CAN WRITE YOUR ANSWERS IN

○ What is the English for VÊ?   _____

○ What is the English for COME?   _____

○ What is the English for QUER?   _____

○ What is the English for TEM?   _____

TURN BACK FOR THE ANSWERS

COVER UP THE LEFT HAND PAGE BEFORE ANSWERING

○ What is the Portuguese for sees? _____

○ What is the Portuguese for eats? _____

○ What is the Portuguese for wants? _____

○ What is the Portuguese for has? _____

TURN BACK FOR THE ANSWERS

Now cover up the answers below and translate the following:

(You can write your answers in)

1. O INSECTO VERDE VÊ A PAREDE FEIA
2. O CAVALO QUER O QUARTO
3. O CAÕ COME O COELHO VELHO
4. O PENTE VÊ O COLCHÃO AZUL
5. A LAGOSTA BRANCA TEM A CADEIRA

The answers are:

1. THE GREEN INSECT SEES THE UGLY WALL
2. THE HORSE WANTS THE ROOM
3. THE DOG EATS THE OLD RABBIT
4. THE COMB SEES THE BLUE MATTRESS
5. THE WHITE LOBSTER HAS THE CHAIR

Now cover up the answers below and translate the following:

(You can write your answers in)

1. THE FLY HAS THE GREEN BLANKET
2. THE SALMON EATS THE YELLOW DOOR
3. THE BRUSH SEES THE FLOOR
4. THE TURKEY HAS THE BLUE HOUSE
5. THE PRAWN WANTS THE RED KITCHEN

The answers are:

1. A MOSCA TEM A MANTA VERDE
2. O SALMÃO COME A PORTA AMARELA
3. A ESCOVA VÊ O CHÃO
4. O PERÚ TEM A CASA AZUL
5. A GAMBA QUER A COZINHA VERMELHA

Section 3 CLOTHES/FAMILY WORDS

CLOTHES

THINK OF EACH IMAGE IN YOUR MIND'S EYE FOR ABOUT TEN SECONDS

○ The Portuguese for HAT is CHAPÉU   (SHAP E O)
  Imagine a hat with a funny SHAPE OH!

○ The Portuguese for COAT is
  SOBRETUDO   (SOOBRETOODOO)
  Imagine you are SO BRAVE TO DO
  anything with your coat on.

○ The Portuguese for TROUSERS is CALÇAS   (KALSASH)
  Imagine COAL ASH over your trousers.

○ The Portuguese for SHIRT is CAMISA   (KAMEEZA)
  Imagine saying, "COME HERE SIR and try
  a shirt on."

○ The Portuguese for BELT is CINTO   (SEENTOO)
  Imagine you need your belt SEEN TO.

○ The Portuguese for SKIRT is SAIA   (SA YA)
  Imagine you SIGH HERE because you can't
  find a nice skirt.

○ The Portuguese for BLOUSE is BLUSA   (BLOOZA)
  Imagine a BLUE blouse.

○ The Portuguese for DRESS is VESTIDO   (VESHTEEDOO)
  Imagine a shopkeeper saying, "I haven't got
  a dress, will a VESTI DO?"

○ The Portuguese for BUTTON is BOTÃO   (BOOTAONG)
  Imagine a BUTTON in a bottle of Port wine.

○ The Portuguese for SCARF is CACHECOL   (CASHKOL)
  Imagine you CATCH COLD without a scarf.

YOU CAN WRITE YOUR ANSWERS IN

○ What is the English for CACHECOL? _____

○ What is the English for BOTÃO? _____

○ What is the English for VESTIDO? _____

○ What is the English for BLUSA? _____

○ What is the English for SAIA? _____

○ What is the English for CINTO? _____

○ What is the English for CAMISA? _____

○ What is the English for CALÇAS? _____

○ What is the English for SOBRETUDO? _____

○ What is the English for CHAPÉU? _____

TURN BACK FOR THE ANSWERS

COVER UP THE LEFT HAND PAGE BEFORE ANSWERING

○ What is the Portuguese for scarf? _____

○ What is the Portuguese for button? _____

○ What is the Portuguese for dress? _____

○ What is the Portuguese for blouse? _____

○ What is the Portuguese for skirt? _____

○ What is the Portuguese for belt? _____

○ What is the Portuguese for shirt? _____

○ What is the Portuguese for trousers? _____

○ What is the Portuguese for coat? _____

○ What is the Portuguese for hat? _____

TURN BACK FOR THE ANSWERS

SOME ADJECTIVES

THINK OF EACH IMAGE IN YOUR MIND'S EYE FOR ABOUT TEN SECONDS

○ The Portuguese for EMPTY is VAZIO   (VAZEE OO)
Imagine the VASE is EMPTY.

○ The Portuguese for HIGH is ALTO   (ALTOO)
Imagine flying at HIGH ALTitudes.

○ The Portuguese for CHEAP is BARATO   (BARATOO)
Imagine a BARITONE being hired for a
CHEAP fee.

○ The Portuguese for EXPENSIVE is CARO   (KAROO)
Imagine buying an EXPENSIVE CAR.

○ The Portuguese for HARD (not soft) is DURO   (DOOROO)
Imagine something HARD and DURABLE.

○ The Portuguese for QUICK is RÁPIDO   (RAPEEDOO)
Imagine being QUICK and RAPID.

○ The Portuguese for EXCELLENT is
EXCELENTE   (ESHLENT)
Imagine EXCELLENT Port wine.

YOU CAN WRITE YOUR ANSWERS IN

O What is the English for EXCELENTE?   _____

O What is the English for RÁPIDO?   _____

O What is the English for DURO?   _____

O What is the English for CARO?   _____

O What is the English for BARATO?   _____

O What is the English for ALTO?   _____

O What is the English for VAZIO?   _____

TURN BACK FOR THE ANSWERS

COVER UP THE LEFT HAND PAGE BEFORE ANSWERING

○ What is the Portuguese for excellent?　　_____

○ What is the Portuguese for quick?　　_____

○ What is the Portuguese are hard?　　_____

○ What is the Portuguese for expensive?　　_____

○ What is the Portuguese for cheap?　　_____

○ What is the Portuguese for high?　　_____

○ What is the Portuguese for empty?　　_____

TURN BACK FOR THE ANSWERS

ELEMENTARY GRAMMAR: AND, BUT and OR

The Portuguese for AND is E (pronounced EE).

Imagine you asked him AND HE answered.

So, CLEAN AND WHITE is LIMPO E BRANCO

The Portuguese for BUT is MAS (pronounced MeSH – remember that a small e is pronounced like the "u" in "curl").

Imagine you like potatoes, BUT not MASHed potatoes.

So, CLEAN BUT WHITE is LIMPO MAS BRANCO

The Portuguese for OR is OU (pronounced O).

Imagine when in pain you either keep quiet OR shout "OH!".

So, CLEAN OR WHITE is LIMPO OU BRANCO

Now cover up the answers below and translate the following:

(You can write your answers in)

1. O PEIXE QUER O CACHECOL MAS O PERÚ QUER O CINTO

2. O CÃO VÊ A CASA VAZIA E O GATO RÁPIDO COME A BLUSA

3. O TOURO PRETO QUER A PAREDE ALTA OU O VESTIDO BARATO

4. O PÁSSARO CANSADO TEM O BOTÃO CARO E O CHAPÉU

5. A VACA AMARELA QUER O SOBRETUDO EXCELENTE

The answers are:

1. THE FISH WANTS THE SCARF BUT THE TURKEY WANTS THE BELT

2. THE DOG SEES THE EMPTY HOUSE AND THE QUICK CAT EATS THE BLOUSE

3. THE BLACK BULL WANTS THE HIGH WALL OR THE CHEAP DRESS

4. THE TIRED BIRD HAS THE EXPENSIVE BUTTON AND THE HAT

5. THE YELLOW COW WANTS THE EXCELLENT COAT

Now cover up the answers below and translate the following:

(You can write your answers in)

1. THE DOG SEES THE WASHBASIN AND THE SHOWER
2. THE GREEN LOBSTER WANTS THE WINDOW OR THE HARD ROOF
3. THE CLEAN CAT HAS THE DIRTY SHIRT AND THE EMPTY TOILET
4. THE BATH IS CLEAN BUT THE BALCONY IS DIRTY
5. THE HORSE HAS TROUSERS AND THE COW WANTS THE SKIRT

The answers are:

1. O CÃO VÊ O LAVATÓRIO E O DUCHE
2. A LAGOSTA VERDE QUER A JANELA OU O TECTO DURO
3. O GATO LIMPO TEM A CAMISA SUJA E A RETRETE VAZIA
4. O BANHO ESTÁ LIMPO MAS A VARANDA ESTÁ SUJA
5. O CAVALO TEM CALÇAS E A VACA QUER A SAIA

FAMILY WORDS

THINK OF EACH IMAGE IN YOUR MIND'S EYE FOR ABOUT TEN SECONDS

O The Portuguese for MOTHER is MÃE   (MAENG)
  Imagine your mother stepped on a MINE.

O The Portuguese for FATHER is PAI   (PA I)
  Imagine throwing a PIE at your father.

O The Portuguese for BROTHER is IRMÃO   (EERMAONG)
  Imagine your brother is an AIRMAN.

O The Portuguese for SISTER is IRMÃ   (EERMANG)
  Imagine your sister is also an AIRMAN – but
  IRMA ends in A not O.

O The Portuguese for HUSBAND is MARIDO   (MAREEDOO)
  Imagine your husband is MARRIED!

O The Portuguese for WIFE is ESPOSA   (ESHPOZA)
  Imagine you EXPOSE your wife as a fraud.

O The Portuguese for SON is FILHO   (FEELYOO)
  Imagine saying to your son, "Let me FEEL
  YOU to see if any bones are broken."

O The Portuguese for DAUGHTER is FILHA   (FEELYA)
  Imagine saying to your daughter, "Let me
  FEEL YA to see if any bones are broken."

O The Portuguese for BOY is RAPAZ   (RAPASH)
  Imagine a boy who wants to WRAP ASH in
  his handkerchief.

O The Portuguese for GIRL is RAPARIGA   (RAPAREEGA)
  Imagine a girl wanting to WRAP HER
  EAGER arms around her dog.

YOU CAN WRITE YOUR ANSWERS IN

○ What is the English for RAPARIGA? _____

○ What is the English for RAPAZ? _____

○ What is the English for FILHA? _____

○ What is the English for FILHO? _____

○ What is the English for ESPOSA? _____

○ What is the English for MARIDO? _____

○ What is the English for IRMÃ? _____

○ What is the English for IRMÃO? _____

○ What is the English for PAI? _____

○ What is the English for MÃE? _____

TURN BACK FOR THE ANSWERS

COVER UP THE LEFT HAND PAGE BEFORE ANSWERING

○ What is the Portuguese for girl?   _____

○ What is the Portuguese for boy?   _____

○ What is the Portuguese for daughter?   _____

○ What is the Portuguese for son?   _____

○ What is the Portuguese for wife?   _____

○ What is the Portuguese for husband?   _____

○ What is the Portuguese for sister?   _____

○ What is the Portuguese for brother?   _____

○ What is the Portuguese for father?   _____

○ What is the Portuguese for mother?   _____

TURN BACK FOR THE ANSWERS

ELEMENTARY GRAMMAR

The next little piece of grammar is about the word "A".

The Portuguese for A (as in A DOG, AN INSECT, A CAT, and so on) is UM (pronounced OONG).

So,

A DOG is UM CÃO

AN INSECT is UM INSECTO

A CAT is UM GATO

When the word is feminine (as in A COW, A FLY, A TABLE, and so on) then A is UMA (pronounced OOMA).

So,

A COW is UMA VACA

A FLY is UMA MOSCA

A TABLE is UMA MESA

Now cover up the answers below and translate the following:

(You can write your answers in)

1. O RAPAZ SUJO QUER UMA CAMISA LIMPA
2. O PAI TEM UM FILHO E UMA FILHA
3. O CHÃO ESTÁ SUJO MAS A ESCOVA ESTÁ LIMPA
4. A MÃE QUER UMA COZINHA OU UMA VARANDA
5. O IRMÃO VÊ UM DUCHE EXCELENTE MAS O TECTO ESTÁ VERDE

The answers are:

1. THE DIRTY BOY WANTS A CLEAN SHIRT
2. THE FATHER HAS A SON AND A DAUGHTER
3. THE FLOOR IS DIRTY BUT THE BRUSH IS CLEAN
4. THE MOTHER WANTS A KITCHEN OR A BALCONY
5. THE BROTHER SEES AN EXCELLENT SHOWER BUT THE ROOF IS GREEN

Now cover up the answers below and translate the following:

(You can write your answers in)

1. A GIRL HAS A HARD HAT
2. THE MOTHER EATS THE QUICK LOBSTER BUT THE FATHER EATS A PRAWN
3. THE SISTER WANTS AN EXPENSIVE SCARF OR A CHEAP BELT
4. THE BROTHER WANTS A WIFE AND THE HUSBAND WANTS A DAUGHTER
5. THE SON HAS A SKIRT BUT THE GIRL HAS TROUSERS

The answers are:

1. UMA RAPARIGA TEM UM CHAPÉU DURO
2. A MÃE COME A LAGOSTA RÁPIDA MAS O PAI COME UMA GAMBA
3. A IRMÃ QUER UM CACHECOL CARO OU UM CINTO BARATO
4. O IRMÃO QUER UMA ESPOSA E O MARIDO QUER UMA FILHA
5. O FILHO TEM UMA SAIA MAS A RAPARIGA TEM CALÇAS

SOME GENERALLY USEFUL WORDS

THINK OF EACH IMAGE IN YOUR MIND'S EYE FOR ABOUT TEN SECONDS

○ The Portuguese for ADDRESS is
  DIRRECÇÃO   (DEERESAONG)
  Imagine asking which DIRECTION
  someone's address is in.

○ The Portuguese for BABY is BEBÉ   (BEBE)
  Imagine pouring Port wine over a BABY.

○ The Portuguese for BATHROOM is
  CASA DE BANHO (f)   (KAZAD BANYOO)
  Imagine you are annoyed 'CAUSE THEY
  BAN YOU from your bathroom.

○ The Portuguese for BONE is OSSO   (OSOO)
  Imagine your bones are OH SO sore.

○ The Portuguese for BOTTLE is GARRAFA   (GARRAFA)
  Imagine a GIRAFFE swallowing a bottle.

○ The Portuguese for BRIDGE is PONTE (f)   (PONT)
  Imagine you POINT to a bridge.

○ The Portuguese for BUILDING is
  EDIFÍCIO   (EDEEFEESYOO)
  Imagine a building with a magnificent
  EDIFICE.

○ The Portuguese for (TIN) CAN is LATA   (LATA)
  Imagine a LETTER sticking out of a tin can.

○ The Portuguese for CITY is CIDADE (f)   (SEEDAD)
  Imagine you SEE DAD in the city.

○ The Portuguese for CORK is ROLHA   (ROLYA)
  Imagine you ROLL YOUR cork over the floor.

YOU CAN WRITE YOUR ANSWERS IN

○ What is the English for ROLHA?   _____

○ What is the English for CIDADE (f)?   _____

○ What is the English for LATA?   _____

○ What is the English for EDIFÍCIO?   _____

○ What is the English for PONTE (f)?   _____

○ What is the English for GARRAFA?   _____

○ What is the English for OSSO?   _____

○ What is the English for CASA DE
BANHO (f)?   _____

○ What is the English for BEBÉ?   _____

○ What is the English for DIRECÇÃO (f)?   _____

TURN BACK FOR THE ANSWERS

COVER UP THE LEFT HAND PAGE BEFORE ANSWERING

○ What is the Portuguese for cork? _____

○ What is the Portuguese for city? _____

○ What is the Portuguese for (tin) can? _____

○ What is the Portuguese for building? _____

○ What is the Portuguese for bridge? _____

○ What is the Portuguese for bottle? _____

○ What is the Portuguese for bone? _____

○ What is the Portuguese for bathroom? _____

○ What is the Portuguese for baby? _____

○ What is the Portuguese for address? _____

TURN BACK FOR THE ANSWERS

Now cover up the answers below and translate the following:

(You can write your answers in)

1. O RAPAZ VÊ UMA CASA DE BANHO E UM TAPETE
   (N.B. CASA DE BANHO is feminine, because CASA is feminine.)

2. A CIDADE ESTÁ VAZIA MAS SUJA

3. A RAPARIGA QUER UMA BLUSA BARATA E UM BOTÃO BRANCO

4. A IRMÃ COME A ROLHA PEQUENA

5. O BEBÉ VÊ O EDIFÍCIO VAZIO

The answers are:

1. THE BOY SEES A BATHROOM AND A RUG

2. THE CITY IS EMPTY BUT DIRTY

3. THE GIRL WANTS A CHEAP BLOUSE AND A WHITE BUTTON

4. THE SISTER EATS THE SMALL CORK

5. THE BABY SEES THE EMPTY BUILDING

Now cover up the answers below and translate the following:

(You can write your answers in)

1. THE GIRL WANTS A HIGH BUILDING, AN EMPTY ROOM AND A BALCONY

2. A BABY WANTS A BONE AND A SHELF

3. THE WIFE WANTS THE ADDRESS

4. THE SON SEES A CORK BUT THE DAUGHTER SEES A BOTTLE AND A TAP

5. A HORSE EATS THE TIN CAN AND A BRIDGE

The answers are:

1. A RAPARIGA QUER UM EDIFÍCIO ALTO, UM QUARTO VAZIO E UMA VARANDA

2. UM BEBÉ QUER UM OSSO E UMA PRATELEIRA

3. A ESPOSA QUER A DIRECÇÃO

4. O FILHO VÊ UMA ROLHA MAS A FILHA VÊ UMA GARRAFA E UMA TORNEIRA

5. UM CAVALO COME A LATA E UMA PONTE

Section 4 IN THE COUNTRY/TIME WORDS, DAYS OF THE WEEK

IN THE COUNTRY

THINK OF EACH IMAGE IN YOUR MIND'S EYE FOR ABOUT TEN SECONDS

○ The Portuguese for GARDEN is JARDIM   (jARDEENG)*
Imagine you JARRED HIM in the garden.

○ The Portuguese for PATH is CAMINHO   (KAMEENYOO)
Imagine shouting to someone on your path,
"COME IN YOU!"

○ The Portuguese for FLOWER is FLOR (f)   (FLOR)
Imagine flowers on the FLOOR.

○ The Portuguese for TREE is ÁRVORE (f)   (ARVOOR)
Imagine trees lining a HARBOUR.

○ The Portuguese for FRUIT is FRUTA   (FROOTA)
Imagine stuffing FRUIT into a bottle of Port
wine.

○ The Portuguese for VEGETABLE is
LEGUME   (LEGOOM)
Imagine you LAY GUM all round the
vegetables in your garden.

○ The Portuguese for PLANT is PLANTA   (PLANTA)
Imagine you put PLANTS into a bottle of
Port wine.

○ The Portuguese for ROCK is ROCHA   (ROSHA)
Imagine RUSSIA is full of rocks.

○ The Portuguese for BUCKET is BALDE   (BAHLD)
Imagine a BALD man with a bucket.

○ The Portuguese for GRASS is RELVA   (RELVA)
Imagine grass has REAL Value.

*Remember that the small j is pronounced like the "s" in "measure".

81

YOU CAN WRITE YOUR ANSWERS IN

○ What is the English for RELVA? _____

○ What is the English for BALDE? _____

○ What is the English for ROCHA? _____

○ What is the English for PLANTA? _____

○ What is the English for LEGUME? _____

○ What is the English for FRUTA? _____

○ What is the English for ÁRVORE (f)? _____

○ What is the English for FLOR (f)? _____

○ What is the English for CAMINHO? _____

○ What is the English for JARDIM? _____

TURN BACK FOR THE ANSWERS

COVER UP THE LEFT HAND PAGE BEFORE ANSWERING

○ What is the Portuguese for grass? _____

○ What is the Portuguese for bucket? _____

○ What is the Portuguese for rock? _____

○ What is the Portuguese for plant? _____

○ What is the Portuguese for vegetable? _____

○ What is the Portuguese for fruit? _____

○ What is the Portuguese for tree? _____

○ What is the Portuguese for flower? _____

○ What is the Portuguese for path? _____

○ What is the Portuguese for garden? _____

TURN BACK FOR THE ANSWERS

TIME

THINK OF EACH IMAGE IN YOUR MIND'S EYE FOR ABOUT TEN SECONDS

○ The Portuguese for TIME is TEMPO   (TEMPOO)
Imagine keeping time to the TEMPO of the music.

○ The Portuguese for SECOND is SEGUNDO   (SEGOONDOO)
Imagine gulping Port wine every SECOND.

○ The Portuguese for MINUTE is MINUTO   (MEENOOTOO)
Imagine it takes you one MINUTE to finish a whole bottle of Port wine.

○ The Portuguese for HOUR is HORA   (ORA)
Imagine waiting in HORROR for the hour to strike.

○ The Portuguese for DAY is DIA (m)   (DEE A)
Imagine writing home: "DEAR Mum, it's a lovely day!"

○ The Portuguese for WEEK is SEMANA   (SMANA)
Imagine going to learned SEMINARS once a week.

○ The Portuguese for MONTH is MÊS   (MESH)
Imagine getting yourself into a MESS once a month.

○ The Portuguese for YEAR is ANO   (ANOO)
Imagine a year is an ANNUal event.

○ The Portuguese for NIGHT is NOITE (f)   (NOIT)
Imagine you drink Port wine every NIGHT.

○ The Portuguese for MORNING is MANHÃ   (MANYANG)
Imagine meeting a MAN YOU know every morning.

YOU CAN WRITE YOUR ANSWERS IN

○ What is the English for MANHÃ? _____

○ What is the English for NOITE (f)? _____

○ What is the English for ANO? _____

○ What is the English for MÊS? _____

○ What is the English for SEMANA? _____

○ What is the English for DIA (m)? _____

○ What is the English for HORA? _____

○ What is the English for MINUTO? _____

○ What is the English for SEGUNDO? _____

○ What is the English for TEMPO? _____

TURN BACK FOR THE ANSWERS

○ What is the Portuguese for morning? _____

○ What is the Portuguese for night? _____

○ What is the Portuguese for year? _____

○ What is the Portuguese for month? _____

○ What is the Portuguese for week? _____

○ What is the Portuguese for day? _____

○ What is the Portuguese for hour? _____

○ What is the Portuguese for minute? _____

○ What is the Portuguese for second? _____

○ What is the Portuguese for time? _____

TURN BACK FOR THE ANSWERS

SOME USEFUL WORDS

THINK OF EACH IMAGE IN YOUR MIND'S EYE FOR ABOUT TEN SECONDS

○ The Portuguese for ALREADY is JÁ   (jA)*
  Imagine JAM ALREADY on your bread.

○ The Portuguese for ALWAYS is SEMPRE   (SENGPR)
  Imagine you ALWAYS SIMPER.

○ The Portuguese for GOOD is BOM   (BONG)
  Imagine feeling GOOD after you BONG your
  drum.

○ The Portuguese for BIG is GRANDE   (GRAND)
  Imagine a BIG GRAND piano.

*Remember that the small j is pronounced like the "s" in "measure".

YOU CAN WRITE YOUR ANSWERS IN

○ What is the English for GRANDE? _____

○ What is the English for BOM? _____

○ What is the English for SEMPRE? _____

○ What is the English for JÁ? _____

TURN BACK FOR THE ANSWERS

COVER UP THE LEFT HAND PAGE BEFORE ANSWERING

○ What is the Portuguese for big? _____

○ What is the Portuguese for good? _____

○ What is the Portuguese for always? _____

○ What is the Portuguese for already? _____

TURN BACK FOR THE ANSWERS

ELEMENTARY GRAMMAR

In Section 1 you learned that the Portuguese for IS is ESTÁ.

However, in Portuguese there are two words for IS – ESTÁ and É (which is pronounced E).

You use ESTÁ for something temporary, and É for something permanent.

For example, if you mean by THE DOG IS QUIET that it is a quiet kind of dog, that its temperament is quiet, and so on, then the Portuguese is O CÃO É TRANQUILO.

If, on the other hand, you mean that the dog is quiet at the moment, that it is being quiet now, and so on, then the Portuguese is O CÃO ESTÁ TRANQUILO.

If you say something like THE TABLE IS SMALL, then it is likely that this is going to be a permanent feature of the table, and this would almost certainly be A MESA É PEQUENA.

If, on the other hand, you add the word TODAY or the word NOW, then this will almost always mean that the state is a temporary one.

The Portuguese for NOW is AGORA (pronounced AGORA)

> Imagine I GORE A bull NOW.

The Portuguese for TODAY is HOJE (pronounced Oj)*

> Imagine doing an ODD job TODAY.

So,

> THE CAT IS TIRED TODAY is O GATO ESTÁ CANSADO HOJE

> THE DOG IS QUIET NOW is O CÃO ESTÁ TRANQUILO AGORA

You must not worry if you do not get this quite right, since it is about the hardest part of the grammar.

In some of the sentences that you will be translating, either É or ESTÁ may be possible – although only one of them will be given.

All you need to remember at this stage is why É and ESTÁ are different.

*Remember that the small j is pronounced like the "s" in "measure".

Now cover up the answers below and translate the following:

(You can write your answers in)

1. HOJE O RAPAZ ESTÁ SUJO
2. O QUARTO ESTÁ VAZIO
3. A PONTE É EXCELENTE
4. O EDIFÍCIO É ALTO E A RELVA É VERDE
5. A SAIA JÁ É CARA

PLEASE NOTE: JÁ usually comes before É or ESTÁ: "already is" rather than "is already".

The answers are:

1. TODAY THE BOY IS DIRTY
2. THE ROOM IS EMPTY
3. THE BRIDGE IS EXCELLENT
4. THE BUILDING IS HIGH AND THE GRASS IS GREEN
5. THE SKIRT IS ALREADY EXPENSIVE

Now cover up the answers below and translate the following:

(You can write your answers in)

1. THE COW IS DIRTY (it is a dirty kind of cow)
2. THE TURKEY IS DIRTY (e.g. it has fallen into some mud)
3. THE FLY IS QUIET NOW
4. THE DUCK IS TIRED TODAY
5. THE DOG IS BLACK AND THE PLANT IS RED

The answers are:

1. A VACA É SUJA
2. O PERÚ ESTÁ SUJO
3. A MOSCA ESTÁ TRANQUILA AGORA
4. O PATO ESTÁ CANSADO HOJE
5. O CÃO É PRETO E A PLANTA É VERMELHA

ELEMENTARY GRAMMAR

PLURALS

Plurals in Portuguese are very simple.

Nouns that end in a vowel usually simply add an "S" (pronounced SH).

So,

> GATO is CAT and GATOS is CATS
>
> VACA is COW and VACAS is COWS

If the noun does not end in a vowel, then you add ES.

For example,

> FLOR is FLOWER, and FLORES is FLOWERS
>
> MÊS is MONTH, and MESES is MONTHS
>
> (the accent is missed off in the plural of this word).

If the noun is plural, then the word for THE has to change too:

> O (the) becomes OS (pronounced OOSH)
>
> A (the) becomes AS (pronounced eSH)*

So,

> THE CATS is OS GATOS (OOSH GATOOSH)
>
> THE COWS is AS VACAS (eSH VAKASH)
>
> THE FLOWERS is AS FLORES (eSH FLORSH)
>
> THE MONTHS is OS MESES (OOSH MEZeSH)

*Remember that the small e is pronounced like the "u" in "curl".

Now cover up the answers below and translate the following:

(You can write your answers in)

1. O GANSO JÁ QUER O JARDIM E OS CAMINHOS
2. O BALDE GRANDE É PRETO
3. UM SALMÃO JÁ VÊ OS MOSQUITOS
4. O MARIDO TEM AS ESCOVAS E OS PENTES
5. O BOM BEBÉ COME SEMPRE OS LEGUMES

The answers are:

1. THE GOOSE ALREADY WANTS THE GARDEN AND THE PATHS
2. THE BIG BUCKET IS BLACK
3. A SALMON ALREADY SEES THE MOSQUITOS
4. THE HUSBAND HAS THE BRUSHES AND THE COMBS
5. THE GOOD BABY ALWAYS EATS THE VEGETABLES

Now cover up the answers below and translate the following:

(You can write your answers in)

1. THE UGLY BOY HAS THE COWS AND THE BULLS
2. THE HOURS, THE MINUTES, THE SECONDS, THE MONTHS OR THE YEARS . . .
3. THE FREE GIRL SEES THE NIGHTS AND THE MORNINGS
4. THE FATHER WANTS THE ROCKS, THE FRUIT OR THE FLOWERS
5. THE MOTHER ALWAYS EATS THE TREES AND THE GRASS

The answers are:

1. O RAPAZ FEIO TEM AS VACAS E OS TOUROS
2. AS HORAS, OS MINUTOS, OS SEGUNDOS, OS MESES OU OS ANOS . . .
3. A RAPARIGA LIVRE VÊ AS NOITES E AS MANHÃS
4. O PAI QUER AS ROCHAS, A FRUTA OU AS FLORES
5. A MÃE COME SEMPRE AS ÁRVORES E A RELVA

DAYS OF THE WEEK

THINK OF EACH IMAGE IN YOUR MIND'S EYE FOR ABOUT TEN SECONDS

With the days of the week from Monday to Friday, the FEIRA can be missed out, though we've mentioned it so you'll recognise it if you see it.

○ The Portuguese for MONDAY is
SEGUNDA-FEIRA   (SEGOONDA FEIRA)
Imagine you count the SECONDS till
MONDAY comes.

○ The Portuguese for TUESDAY is
TERÇA-FEIRA   (TERSA FEIRA)
Imagine TEARS Appear in your eyes when
TUESDAY arrives.

○ The Portuguese for WEDNESDAY is
QUARTA-FEIRA   (KWARTA FEIRA)
Imagine WEDNESDAY feels like
QUARTER way through the week.

○ The Portuguese for THURSDAY is
QUINTA-FEIRA   (KEENTA FEIRA)
Imagine you're KEEN TO see
THURSDAYS.

○ The Portuguese for FRIDAY is
SEXTA-FEIRA   (SESHTA FEIRA)
Imagine a SEX STAR arriving on FRIDAY
for a concert.

○ The Portuguese for SATURDAY is SÁBADO   (SABADOO)
Imagine SATURDAY is the Jewish
SABBATH.

○ The Portuguese for SUNDAY is DOMINGO (DOOMEENGOO)
Imagine DOMINICAN monks pray on a
SUNDAY.

YOU CAN WRITE YOUR ANSWERS IN

○ What is the English for DOMINGO? _____

○ What is the English for SÁBADO? _____

○ What is the English for SEXTA-FEIRA? _____

○ What is the English for QUINTA-FEIRA? _____

○ What is the English for QUARTA-FEIRA? _____

○ What is the English for TERÇA-FEIRA? _____

○ What is the English for SEGUNDA-
FEIRA? _____

TURN BACK FOR THE ANSWERS

COVER UP THE LEFT HAND PAGE BEFORE ANSWERING

○ What is the Portuguese for Sunday? _____

○ What is the Portuguese for Saturday? _____

○ What is the Portuguese for Friday? _____

○ What is the Portuguese for Thursday? _____

○ What is the Portuguese for Wednesday? _____

○ What is the Portuguese for Tuesday? _____

○ What is the Portuguese for Monday? _____

TURN BACK FOR THE ANSWERS

ELEMENTARY GRAMMAR

To say ON FRIDAY(S), ON MONDÀY(S), and so on, you use the word ÀS (pronounced ASH) to mean ON.

So, ON THURSDAY is ÀS QUINTAS (ASH KEENTASH)

  Remember ASH WEDNESDAY.

But with DOMINGO (Sunday) and SÁBADO (Saturday) you say AOS (pronounced A OOSH).

So, ON SUNDAYS is AOS DOMINGOS

Now cover up the answers below and translate the following:

(You can write your answers in)

1. UMA VACA GRANDE JÁ TEM AS FLORES SUJAS E AS PLANTAS
2. ÀS QUINTAS A CASA ESTÁ VAZIA
3. A LAGOSTA ESTÁ SUJA HOJE
4. O MARIDO ESTÁ LIVRE AOS SÁBADOS
5. AOS DOMINGOS O PATO COME RELVA

The answers are:

1. A BIG COW ALREADY HAS THE DIRTY FLOWERS AND THE PLANTS
2. ON THURSDAYS THE HOUSE IS EMPTY
3. THE LOBSTER IS DIRTY TODAY
4. THE HUSBAND IS FREE ON SATURDAYS
5. ON SUNDAYS THE DUCK EATS GRASS

Now cover up the answers below and translate the following:

(You can write your answers in)

1. THE WIFE EATS FRUIT ON MONDAYS AND TUESDAYS
2. THE CAT IS QUIET TODAY
3. THE BIG BOY SEES THE CITIES ON FRIDAYS
4. THE NIGHT IS ALWAYS BLACK ON WEDNESDAYS
5. ON SATURDAYS A GOOD GIRL WANTS BIG VEGETABLES

The answers are:

1. A ESPOSA COME FRUTA ÀS SEGUNDAS E ÀS TERÇAS
2. O GATO ESTÀ TRANQUILO HOJE
3. O RAPAZ GRANDE VÊ AS CIDADES ÀS SEXTAS
4. A NOITE É SEMPRE PRETA ÀS QUARTAS
5. AOS SÁBADOS UMA BOA RAPARIGA QUER LEGUMES GRANDES

Please note: you probably put BOM for GOOD in the last sentence. But BOM becomes BOA (pronounced BOA) with a feminine word.

Note also that BOM and BOA often come BEFORE the word they describe.

ELEMENTARY GRAMMAR

In Portuguese you can usually miss out words like "he", "she", "it" and "you".

So, TEM means HAS, but it also means HE or SHE or IT HAS, and YOU HAVE.

The same is true for QUER, COME, VÊ, É, ESTÁ and so on.

So,

HE EATS THE TABLE is COME A MESA

SHE HAS THE FLOWERS is TEM AS FLORES

IT IS THE INSECT is É O INSECTO

YOU WANT A COW is QUER UMA VACA

YOU ARE FREE is ESTÁ LIVRE

and so on.

PLEASE NOTE that ESTÁ and É, when used with "you", mean ARE not IS.

SOME USEFUL WORDS

THINK OF EACH IMAGE IN YOUR MIND'S EYE FOR ABOUT TEN SECONDS

○ The Portuguese for DINNER is JANTAR   (jANTAR)*
  Imagine SANTA Claus eating dinner.

○ The Portuguese for BREAKFAST is
  PEQUENO-ALMOÇO   (PEKEN ALMOSOO)
  Imagine you ALMOST SUE your hotel for the
  little (PEQUENO) they give you for breakfast.

○ The Portuguese for RAIN is CHUVA   (SHOOVA)
  Imagine you SHOVE A grandmother into the
  rain.

○ The Portuguese for SNOW is NEVE (f)   (NEV)
  Imagine they NEVER have snow in Portugal.

○ The Portuguese for THUNDERSTORM is
  TEMPESTADE (f)   (TEMPESHTAD)
  Imagine saying to your father, "That
  thunderstorm sounds like the TEMPEST
  DAD."

○ The Portuguese for DIET is DIETA   (DEE ETA)
  Imagine THEY EAT A lot when they use
  diets in Portugal.

○ The Portuguese for ELEVATOR (LIFT) is
  ELEVADOR   (EELVADOR)
  Imagine an ELEVATOR loaded with bottles
  of port wine.

○ The Portuguese for FLOOR (STOREY) is
  ANDAR   (ANDAR)
  Imagine you live UNDER the second floor.

○ The Portuguese for FOOD is COMIDA   (KOOMEEDA)
  Imagine eating food in Portugal is a
  COMEDY.

○ The Portuguese for HARBOUR is PORTO   (PORTOO)
  Imagine a harbour – a large PORT – not
  Port wine!

*A last reminder that the small j is pronounced like the "s" in "measure".

107

YOU CAN WRITE YOUR ANSWERS IN

○ What is the English for PORTO? _____

○ What is the English for COMIDA? _____

○ What is the English for ANDAR? _____

○ What is the English for ELEVADOR? _____

○ What is the English for DIETA? _____

○ What is the English for TEMPESTADE (f)? _____

○ What is the English for NEVE (f)? _____

○ What is the English for CHUVA? _____

○ What is the English for
PEQUENO-ALMOÇO? _____

○ What is the English for JANTAR? _____

TURN BACK FOR THE ANSWERS

COVER UP THE LEFT HAND PAGE BEFORE ANSWERING

○ What is the Portuguese for harbour? _____

○ What is the Portuguese for food? _____

○ What is the Portuguese for floor (storey)? _____

○ What is the Portuguese for elevator (lift)? _____

○ What is the Portuguese for diet? _____

○ What is the Portuguese for thunderstorm? _____

○ What is the Portuguese for snow? _____

○ What is the Portuguese for rain? _____

○ What is the Portuguese for breakfast? _____

○ What is the Portuguese for dinner? _____

TURN BACK FOR THE ANSWERS

Now cover up the answers below and translate the following:

(You can write your answers in)

1. É O INSECTO AMARELO MAS JÁ ESTÁ GRANDE
2. VÊ O ELEVADOR. É VELHO
3. COME O PEQUENO-ALMOÇO E VÊ A TEMPESTADE
4. ÀS SEGUNDAS QUER SEMPRE UMA PLANTA
5. AOS SÁBADOS COME A RELVA AZUL

The answers are:

1. IT IS THE YELLOW INSECT BUT IT IS ALREADY BIG
2. YOU SEE THE LIFT. IT IS OLD.
3. SHE EATS THE BREAKFAST AND SEES THE
   THUNDERSTORM
4. ON MONDAYS YOU ALWAYS WANT A PLANT
5. ON SATURDAYS HE EATS THE BLUE GRASS

PLEASE NOTE that in translating these sentences, "he", "she",
"you" and "it" are interchangeable, so you were not wrong if you
put "he" instead of "you" etc.

This will apply from now on in this course when you are translating
from Portuguese into English.

Now cover up the answers below and translate the following:

(You can write your answers in)

1. YOU EAT THE FOOD ON SUNDAYS
2. SHE SEES THE HARBOUR
3. HE WANTS THE SNOW AND THE RAIN
4. IT IS A GOOD DINNER BUT YOU ARE TIRED
5. IT IS A GOOD DIET

The answers are:

1. COME A COMIDA AOS DOMINGOS
2. VÊ O PORTO
3. QUER A NEVE E A CHUVA
4. É UM BOM JANTAR MAS ESTÁ CANSADO
5. É UMA BOA DIETA

Section 5   IN THE RESTAURANT, NUMBERS, FOOD AND DRINK, TELLING THE TIME

IN THE RESTAURANT

THINK OF EACH IMAGE IN YOUR MIND'S EYE FOR ABOUT TEN SECONDS

○ The Portuguese for RESTAURANT is
RESTAURANTE   (ReSHTA OORANT)*
Imagine a RESTAURANT serving
nothing but bottles of Port wine.

○ The Portuguese for KNIFE is FACA   (FAKA)
Imagine an Indian FAKIR stabbing himself
with a knife.

○ The Portuguese for FORK is GARFO   (GARFOO)
Imagine your CAR FULL of forks.

○ The Portuguese for SPOON is COLHER (f)   (KOOLYER)
Imagine you COOL your egg with a spoon.

○ The Portuguese for PLATE is PRATO   (PRATOO)
Imagine a baby PRATTling as it throws a
plate at you.

○ The Portuguese for MENU is MENÚ   (MENOO)
Imagine a large number of different kinds of
Port wine listed on the MENU.

○ The Portuguese for NAPKIN is
GUARDANAPO   (GWARDANAPOO)
Imagine you GUARD A NAPkin with your
life.

○ The Portuguese for SERVICE is SERVIÇO   (SeRVEESOO)*
Imagine asking for SERVICE SOOn.

○ The Portuguese for BILL is CONTA   (KONTA)
Imagine trying to CONTAct your waiter so he
can give you the bill.

○ The Portuguese for CUP is CHÁVENA   (SHAVNA)
Imagine you SHAVE IN A cup.

*Remember that the small e is pronounced like the "u" in "curl".

113

YOU CAN WRITE YOUR ANSWERS IN

○ What is the English for CHÁVENA? _____

○ What is the English for CONTA? _____

○ What is the English for SERVIÇO? _____

○ What is the English for GUARDANAPO? _____

○ What is the English for MENÚ? _____

○ What is the English for PRATO? _____

○ What is the English for COLHER (f)? _____

○ What is the English for GARFO? _____

○ What is the English for FACA? _____

○ What is the English for RESTAURANTE? _____

TURN BACK FOR THE ANSWERS

COVER UP THE LEFT HAND PAGE BEFORE ANSWERING

○ What is the Portuguese for cup? _____

○ What is the Portuguese for bill? _____

○ What is the Portuguese for service? _____

○ What is the Portuguese for napkin? _____

○ What is the Portuguese for menu? _____

○ What is the Portuguese for plate? _____

○ What is the Portuguese for spoon? _____

○ What is the Portuguese for fork? _____

○ What is the Portuguese for knife? _____

○ What is the Portuguese for restaurant? _____

TURN BACK FOR THE ANSWERS

ELEMENTARY GRAMMAR

The Portuguese for ARE is SÃO (pronounced SAONG) if the state is permanent, or ESTÃO (pronounced ESHTAONG) if the state is temporary.

So,

> THE DOG AND THE CAT ARE QUIET
> (they are both of a quiet temperament)

> is O CÃO E O GATO SÃO TRANQUILOS.

> > THE DOG AND THE CAT ARE QUIET TODAY

> is O CÃO E O GATO ESTÃO TRANQUILOS HOJE
> (temporary state).

Note that you have to make the adjective plural too.

So,

> TRANQUILO becomes TRANQUILOS.

Whenever you make an adjective plural, you simply add an "S" (pronounced SH).

So,

> TRANQUILAS is the feminine plural.

LIVRES is the plural of LIVRE in both the masculine and feminine.

You should also note that when an adjective goes with TWO words which are of different genders, then it becomes MASCULINE and PLURAL.

In other words, the masculine dominates the feminine!

So,

> THE DOG AND THE COW ARE BLACK
> is O CÃO E A VACA SÃO PRETOS.

Now cover up the answers below and translate the following:

(You can write your answers in)

1. A COLHER É GRANDE E AS GARRAFAS SÃO VELHAS
2. ÀS CHÁVENAS ESTÃO VAZIAS
3. AOS SABADOS O RAPAZ COME AS CONTAS
4. HOJE OS RELÓGIOS BRANCOS ESTÃO LIMPOS
5. OS POLVOS E OS COELHOS ESTÃO TRANQUILOS

The answers are:

1. THE SPOON IS BIG AND THE BOTTLES ARE OLD
2. THE CUPS ARE EMPTY
3. ON SATURDAYS THE BOY EATS THE BILLS
4. TODAY THE WHITE CLOCKS ARE CLEAN
5. THE OCTOPUSES AND THE RABBITS ARE QUIET

Now cover up the answers below and translate the following:

(You can write your answers in)

1. THE RESTAURANTS ARE SMALL
2. THE HUSBAND AND THE WIFE ARE ALREADY TIRED
3. THE KNIVES AND THE FORKS ARE CHEAP
4. THE MENU AND THE SERVICE ARE EXCELLENT
5. THE NAPKINS ARE RED BUT THE PLATES ARE GREEN

The answers are:

1. OS RESTAURANTES SÃO PEQUENOS
2. O MARIDO E A ESPOSA JÁ ESTÃO CANSADOS
3. AS FACAS E OS GARFOS SÃO BARATOS
4. O MENÚ E O SERVIÇO SÃO EXCELENTES
5. OS GUARDANAPOS SÃO VERMELHOS MAS OS PRATOS SÃO VERDES

NUMBERS

THINK OF EACH IMAGE IN YOUR MIND'S EYE FOR ABOUT TEN SECONDS

○ The Portuguese for ONE is UM   (OONG)
Imagine ONE bottle of Port wine.

○ The Portuguese for TWO is DOIS   (DOISH)
Imagine you TOSS TWO coins in the air.

○ The Portuguese for THREE is TRÊS   (TRESH)
Imagine you TREASure THREE blind mice.

○ The Portuguese for FOUR is QUATRO   (KWATROO)
Imagine FOUR QUARTERS.

○ The Portuguese for FIVE is CINCO   (SEENKOO)
Imagine asking FIVE Scotsmen, "Have you
SEEN KOOS (cows)?"

○ The Portuguese for SIX is SEIS   (SEISH)
Imagine someone SAYS SIX, six times.

○ The Portuguese for SEVEN is SETE   (SET)
Imagine playing SEVEN SETS at tennis.

○ The Portuguese for EIGHT is OITO   (OITOO)
Imagine I TOO look EIGHT years old.

○ The Portuguese for NINE is NOVE   (NOV)
Imagine a German saying, "NO Vay (way) will
I dial 999."

○ The Portuguese for ZERO is ZERO   (ZEROO)
Imagine an empty bottle of Port wine with
ZERO port in it.

YOU CAN WRITE YOUR ANSWERS IN

○ What is the English for ZERO? _____

○ What is the English for NOVE? _____

○ What is the English for OITO? _____

○ What is the English for SETE? _____

○ What is the English for SEIS? _____

○ What is the English for CINCO? _____

○ What is the English for QUATRO? _____

○ What is the English for TRÊS? _____

○ What is the English for DOIS? _____

○ What is the English for UM? _____

TURN BACK FOR THE ANSWERS

COVER UP THE LEFT HAND PAGE BEFORE ANSWERING

○ What is the Portuguese for zero? _____

○ What is the Portuguese for nine? _____

○ What is the Portuguese for eight? _____

○ What is the Portuguese for seven? _____

○ What is the Portuguese for six? _____

○ What is the Portuguese for five? _____

○ What is the Portuguese for four? _____

○ What is the Portuguese for three? _____

○ What is the Portuguese for two? _____

○ What is the Portuguese for one? _____

TURN BACK FOR THE ANSWERS

ELEMENTARY GRAMMAR

Most numbers do not change their endings in the way adjectives do. They just stay the same.

So, FIVE COWS is CINCO VACAS

However, UM becomes UMA (pronounced OOMA) before a feminine word – just as it does when it means "A".

Also, DOIS becomes DUAS (pronounced DOO eSH)* before a feminine word.

So, TWO COWS is DUAS VACAS

*Remember that the small e is pronounced like the "u" in "curl".

Now cover up the answers below and translate the following:

(You can write your answers in)

1. OITO SEGUNDOS SÃO UMA HORA
2. A COLHER É FEIA OU VELHA
3. QUATRO SEMANAS SÃO UM MÊS
4. OS PERÚS JÁ ESTÃO CANSADOS
5. DUAS MESAS SÃO CARAS

The answers are:

1. EIGHT SECONDS ARE ONE HOUR
2. THE SPOON IS UGLY OR OLD
3. FOUR WEEKS ARE ONE MONTH
4. THE TURKEYS ARE ALREADY TIRED
5. TWO TABLES ARE EXPENSIVE

Now cover up the answers below and translate the following:

(You can write your answers in)

1. HE SEES NINE FORKS AND SEVEN TABLES
2. SHE HAS TWO ROCKS BUT THE BOY HAS SIX KNIVES
3. SEVEN DAYS ARE ONE WEEK
4. ON FRIDAYS YOU EAT FIVE TREES
5. YOU HAVE THREE FLOWERS

The answers are:

1. VÊ NOVE GARFOS E SETE MESAS
2. TEM DUAS ROCHAS MAS O RAPAZ TEM SEIS FACAS
3. SETE DIAS SÃO UMA SEMANA
4. ÀS SEXTAS COME CINCO ÁRVORES
5. TEM TRÊS FLORES

FOOD AND DRINK

THINK OF EACH IMAGE IN YOUR MIND'S EYE FOR ABOUT TEN SECONDS

○ The Portuguese for WATER is ÁGUA (AGWA)
Imagine an AQUAduct taking water to your
hotel.

○ The Portuguese for WINE is VINHO (VEENYOO)
Imagine a German saying, "VE KNOW what
the best wine is."

○ The Portuguese for COFFEE is CAFÉ (KA FE)
Imagine pouring a bottle of Port wine into a
cup of COFFEE.

○ The Portuguese for MILK is LEITE (LEIT)
Imagine arriving home LATE and being given
a glass of milk.

○ The Portuguese for RICE is ARROZ (ARROSH)
Imagine firing ARROWS which land in a plate
of someone's rice.

○ The Portuguese for BREAD is PÃO (PAONG)
Imagine paying a POUND for a loaf of bread.

○ The Portuguese for BUTTER is MANTEIGA (MANTEIGA)
Imagine you see a MAN TAKE A pack of
butter from a shop.

○ The Portuguese for EGG is OVO (OVOO)
Imagine a chicken has to ovulate eggs.

○ The Portuguese for SALAD is SALADA (SALADA)
Imagine having SALAD with a bottle of Port
wine.

○ The Portuguese for SOUP is SOPA (SOPA)
Imagine drinking soup that tastes like SOAP.

YOU CAN WRITE YOUR ANSWERS IN

○ What is the English for SOPA? _____

○ What is the English for SALADA? _____

○ What is the English for OVO? _____

○ What is the English for MANTEIGA? _____

○ What is the English for PÃO? _____

○ What is the English for ARROZ? _____

○ What is the English for LEITE? _____

○ What is the English for CAFÉ? _____

○ What is the English for VINHO? _____

○ What is the English for ÁGUA? _____

TURN BACK FOR THE ANSWERS

COVER UP THE LEFT HAND PAGE BEFORE ANSWERING

○ What is the Portuguese for soup? _____

○ What is the Portuguese for salad? _____

○ What is the Portuguese for egg? _____

○ What is the Portuguese for butter? _____

○ What is the Portuguese for bread? _____

○ What is the Portuguese for rice? _____

○ What is the Portuguese for milk? _____

○ What is the Portuguese for coffee? _____

○ What is the Portuguese for wine? _____

○ What is the Portuguese for water? _____

TURN BACK FOR THE ANSWERS

Now cover up the answers below and translate the following:

(You can write your answers in)

1. O VINHO É VELHO
2. A MANTEIGA É AMARELA
3. O PAI VÊ A SOPA EXCELENTE
4. ÀS QUARTAS O SERVIÇO É BOM
5. UMA CASA PRETA TEM UM ANDAR

The answers are:

1. THE WINE IS OLD
2. THE BUTTER IS YELLOW
3. THE FATHER SEES THE EXCELLENT SOUP
4. ON WEDNESDAYS THE SERVICE IS GOOD
5. A BLACK HOUSE HAS ONE FLOOR (storey)

Now cover up the answers below and translate the following:

(You can write your answers in)

1. SHE EATS NINE EGGS
2. THE WATER AND THE BREAD ARE EXPENSIVE
3. THE MILK AND THE RICE ARE CHEAP
4. THE SON EATS FIVE SALADS
5. THE COFFEE IS GOOD

The answers are:

1. COME NOVE OVOS
2. A AGUA E O PÃO SÃO CAROS
3. O LEITE E O ARROZ SÃO BARATOS
4. O FILHO COME CINCO SALADAS
5. O CAFÉ É BOM

TELLING THE TIME

THINK OF EACH IMAGE IN YOUR MIND'S EYE FOR ABOUT TEN SECONDS

○ The Portuguese for TEN is DEZ   (DESH)
Imagine you have to DASH at 10 o'clock.

○ The Portuguese for ELEVEN is ONZE   (ONZ)
Imagine eleven footballers ON THE field.

○ The Portuguese for TWENTY is VINTE   (VEENT)
Imagine the 1920s were VINTage years.

○ The Portuguese for TWENTY-FIVE is
VINTE E CINCO   (VEENTESEENKOO)
Imagine VINTE and CINCO – twenty and
five – twenty-five.

○ The Portuguese for QUARTER is QUARTO   (KWARTOO)
Imagine drinking a QUARTER bottle of Port
wine.

○ The Portuguese for HALF is MEIA   (MEIA)
Imagine asking, "MAY I cut you in half?"

○ The Portuguese for MIDDAY is
MEIO-DIA (m)   (ME OO-DEE A)
Imagine saying, "MAY YOU DIE at
midday!"

○ The Portuguese for MIDNIGHT is
MEIA-NOITE (f)   (MEIA-NOIT)
Imagine saying, "MAY YOU NOT do
anything bad after midnight."

○ The Portuguese for LESS is MENOS   (MENOOSH)
Imagine something is less, a MINUS
quantity.

YOU CAN WRITE YOUR ANSWERS IN

○ What is the English for MENOS? _____

○ What is the English for MEIA-NOITE (f)? _____

○ What is the English for MEIO-DIA (m)? _____

○ What is the English for MEIA? _____

○ What is the English for QUARTO? _____

○ What is the English for VINTE E CINCO? _____

○ What is the English for VINTE? _____

○ What is the English for ONZE? _____

○ What is the English for DEZ? _____

TURN BACK FOR THE ANSWERS

COVER UP THE LEFT HAND PAGE BEFORE ANSWERING

○ What is the Portuguese for less? _____

○ What is the Portuguese for midnight? _____

○ What is the Portuguese for midday? _____

○ What is the Portuguese for half? _____

○ What is the Portuguese for quarter? _____

○ What is the Portuguese for twenty-five? _____

○ What is the Portuguese for twenty? _____

○ What is the Portuguese for eleven? _____

○ What is the Portuguese for ten? _____

TURN BACK FOR THE ANSWERS

TELLING THE TIME

As you learned earlier, the Portuguese for HOUR is HORA.
The Portuguese for WHAT is QUE (pronounced KEE).
Imagine thinking, "WHAT KEY is that?"

In Portuguese, to say WHAT TIME IS IT? you say, literally, WHAT HOURS ARE?
That is: QUE HORAS SÃO?
To answer this question in Portuguese, for example IT IS THREE O'CLOCK, IT IS SEVEN O'CLOCK and so on, you say literally THEY ARE THREE HOURS, THEY ARE SEVEN HOURS, etc.
For example:

SÃO TRÊS HORAS

SÃO SETE HORAS.

Since HORA is feminine, IT IS TWO O'CLOCK is SÃO DUAS HORAS.

ONE O'CLOCK is UMA HORA and, of course, IT IS ONE O'CLOCK is É UMA HORA (not SÃO).

The same goes for midday and midnight. So,

IT IS TWELVE O'CLOCK, MIDDAY is É MEIO-DIA

IT IS TWELVE O'CLOCK, MIDNIGHT is É MEIA-
NOITE

Now cover up the answers below and translate the following:

(You can write your answers in)

1. IT IS FIVE O'CLOCK
2. IT IS ONE O'CLOCK
3. IT IS ELEVEN O'CLOCK
4. IT IS TWELVE O'CLOCK, MIDNIGHT
5. IT IS TWO O'CLOCK
6. IT IS NINE O'CLOCK

The answers are:

1. SÃO CINCO HORAS
2. É UMA HORA
3. SÃO ONZE HORAS
4. É MEIA-NOITE
5. SÃO DUAS HORAS
6. SÃO NOVE HORAS

ELEMENTARY GRAMMAR

MORE ON TELLING THE TIME

When you want to say some time TO the hour, or PAST the hour, the first thing to know is that you miss out the word for "hour".

The next thing to know is that you use E (meaning AND) to give the time PAST the hour, saying literally, for example, EIGHT AND FIVE for FIVE PAST EIGHT.

FIVE PAST EIGHT in Portuguese, then, is OITO E CINCO.

Here are some other examples:

IT IS TWENTY PAST TWO is SÃO DUAS E VINTE

IT IS HALF PAST ONE is É UMA E MEIA

You use MENOS (meaning MINUS) to give the time TO the hour.

So, TWENTY-FIVE TO ONE becomes, literally, ONE MINUS TWENTY-FIVE which in Portuguese is UMA MENOS VINTE E CINCO.

TWENTY TO NINE is NOVE MENOS VINTE

TEN TO TWO is DUAS MENOS DEZ

and so on.

The only exception is with QUARTER TO and QUARTER PAST. Here you have to say UM QUARTO instead of just QUARTO.

IT IS QUARTER TO SIX is
SÃO SEIS MENOS UM QUARTO

IT IS QUARTER PAST TWELVE, MIDDAY is
É MEIO-DIA E UM QUARTO.

Now cover up the answers below and translate the following:

(You can write your answers in)

1. IT IS HALF PAST THREE
2. IT IS FOUR O'CLOCK
3. IT IS QUARTER TO TWO
4. IT IS TEN TO SEVEN
5. IT IS QUARTER PAST NINE
6. IT IS TWENTY-FIVE TO ONE
7. IT IS SIX O'CLOCK

The answers are:

1. SÃO TRÊS E MEIA
2. SÃO QUATRO HORAS
3. SÃO DUAS MENOS UM QUARTO
4. SÃO SETE MENOS DEZ
5. SÃO NOVE E UM QUARTO
6. É UMA MENOS VINTE E CINCO
7. SÃO SEIS HORAS

ELEMENTARY GRAMMAR

If you want to say AT ten o'clock, AT a quarter past four, and so on, then in Portuguese you simply say:

ÀS DEZ HORAS, ÀS QUATRO E UM QUARTO, etc.
(ÀS is pronounced ASH).

With the hour ONE, then you use À.

Section 6 MORE FOOD AND DRINK

THINK OF EACH IMAGE IN YOUR MIND'S EYE FOR ABOUT TEN SECONDS

○ The Portuguese for MEAT is CARNE (f)   (KARN)
Imagine CARNivores eating meat.

○ The Portuguese for CHICKEN is FRANGO   (FRANGOO)
Imagine you should always FRANK YOUR
chicken with a date stamp.

○ The Portuguese for GARLIC is ALHO   (ALYOO)
Imagine thinking, "ALL YOU smell of is
garlic."

○ The Portuguese for POTATO is BATATA   (BATATA)
Imagine shouting, "BAT AT HER with
potatoes."

○ The Portuguese for TOMATO is TOMATE   (TOOMAT)
Imagine a bowl of TOMATOES in Port wine.

○ The Portuguese for ICE CREAM is GELADO   (jELADOO)
Imagine thinking, "I'm GLAD YOU bought
me this ice cream to cool me down."

○ The Portuguese for CAKE is BOLO   (BOLOO)
Imagine a cake shaped like a BALLOON.

○ The Portuguese for SALT is SAL   (SAL)
Imagine you SELL salt.

○ The Portuguese for PEPPER is PIMENTA   (PEEMENTA)
Imagine you demand PAYMENT for your
pepper.

○ The Portuguese for DRINK is BEBIDA   (BeBEEDA)
Imagine a BABY DUCK drinking.

YOU CAN WRITE YOUR ANSWERS IN

○ What is the English for BEBIDA? _____

○ What is the English for PIMENTA? _____

○ What is the English for SAL? _____

○ What is the English for BOLO? _____

○ What is the English for GELADO? _____

○ What is the English for TOMATE? _____

○ What is the English for BATATA? _____

○ What is the English for ALHO? _____

○ What is the English for FRANGO? _____

○ What is the English for CARNE (f)? _____

TURN BACK FOR THE ANSWERS

○ What is the Portuguese for drink? _____

○ What is the Portuguese for pepper? _____

○ What is the Portuguese for salt? _____

○ What is the Portuguese for cake? _____

○ What is the Portuguese for ice cream? _____

○ What is the Portuguese for tomato? _____

○ What is the Portuguese for potato? _____

○ What is the Portuguese for garlic? _____

○ What is the Portuguese for chicken? _____

○ What is the Portuguese for meat? _____

TURN BACK FOR THE ANSWERS

SOME USEFUL WORDS

THINK OF EACH IMAGE IN YOUR MIND'S EYE FOR ABOUT TEN SECONDS

○ The Portuguese for ON or IN is EM   (ENG)
  Imagine something ON and IN an ENgine.

○ The Portuguese for UNDER is DEBAIXO
  DE   (DeBAISHOO De)
  Imagine THEY BASH YOU UNDER DE
  table in Portugal.

○ The Portuguese for OUTSIDE is FORA DE   (FORA De)
  Imagine you go OUTSIDE FOR A walk.

○ The Portuguese for BETWEEN is ENTRE   (ENTR)
  Imagine you ENTER BETWEEN two pillars.

YOU CAN WRITE YOUR ANSWERS IN

○ What is the English for ENTRE? _____

○ What is the English for FORA DE? _____

○ What is the English for DEBAIXO DE? _____

○ What is the English for EM? _____

TURN BACK FOR THE ANSWERS

144

COVER UP THE LEFT HAND PAGE BEFORE ANSWERING

○ What is the Portuguese for between? _____

○ What is the Portuguese for outside? _____

○ What is the Portuguese for under? _____

○ What is the Portuguese for on or in? _____

TURN BACK FOR THE ANSWERS

ELEMENTARY GRAMMAR

You have just been given some "position" words (sometimes called "prepositions").

With position, "is" and "are" are used frequently in Portuguese as you would expect.

É and SÃO indicate permanent position, and ESTÁ and ESTÃO temporary position.

LISBON IS IN PORTUGAL is LISBOA É EM PORTUGAL

(LISBOA – pronounced LEESBOA – is the Portuguese for Lisbon).

HE IS UNDER THE TABLE NOW is ESTÁ DEBAIXO DA MESA AGORA

You probably noticed in the last sentence that DE (in DEBAIXO DE) plus A (THE) became DA.

The same kind of thing happens when DE comes before any of the Portuguese words for THE and A or AN. The DE loses its E and the two words become one.

So,

DE plus O	becomes DO (DOO)
DE plus A	becomes DA (De)
DE plus OS	becomes DOS (DOOSH)
DE plus AS	becomes DAS (DeSH)
DE plus UM	becomes DUM (DOONG)
DE plus UMA	becomes DUMA (DOOMA)

The same sort of thing happens with EM (IN or ON), except that EM becomes N and the two words become one.

So,

EM plus O	becomes NO (NOO)
EM plus A	becomes NA (Ne)
EM plus OS	becomes NOS (NOOSH)
EM plus AS	becomes NAS (NeSH)
EM plus UM	becomes NUM (NOONG)
EM plus UMA	becomes NUMA (NOOMA)

So, for example,

ON THE TABLE is	NA MESA
ON THE FLOOR is	NO CHÃO
IN THE HOUSE is	NA CASA

Now cover up the answers below and translate the following:

(You can write your answers in)

1. O IRMÃO FEIO COME UMA BATATA, UM GELADO E UM BOLO

2. O ALHO ESTÁ NA BEBIDA

3. SEIS CHÁVENAS ESTÃO NO ARMÁRIO

4. O RELÓGIO ESTÁ NUMA GAVETA MAS A MANTA ESTÁ NO CHÃO

5. A COZINHA É NA CASA

The answers are:

1. THE UGLY BROTHER EATS A POTATO, AN ICE CREAM AND A CAKE

2. THE GARLIC IS IN THE DRINK

3. SIX CUPS ARE IN THE CUPBOARD

4. THE CLOCK IS IN A DRAWER, BUT THE BLANKET IS ON THE FLOOR

5. THE KITCHEN IS IN THE HOUSE

Now cover up the answers below and translate the following:

(You can write your answers in)

1. THE MEAT AND THE CHICKEN ARE ON THE TABLE
2. THE SALT AND THE PEPPER ARE UNDER A TOMATO
3. THE CHAIR IS OUTSIDE THE BUILDING
4. THE BALCONY IS OUTSIDE THE HOUSE
5. THE BRIDGE IS BETWEEN THE HOUSE AND THE CITY

The answers are:

1. A CARNE E O FRANGO ESTÃO NA MESA
2. O SAL E A PIMENTA ESTÃO DEBAIXO DUM TOMATE
3. A CADEIRA ESTÁ FORA DO EDIFÍCIO
4. A VARANDA É FORA DA CASA
5. A PONTE É ENTRE A CASA E A CIDADE

MORE FOOD

THINK OF EACH IMAGE IN YOUR MIND'S EYE FOR ABOUT TEN SECONDS

○ The Portuguese for TUNNY is ATUM   (ATOONG)
Imagine a tunny fish splitting the ATOM.

○ The Portuguese for ANCHOVY is ANCHOVA   (ANSHOVA)
Imagine ANCHOVIES in Port wine.

○ The Portuguese for LETTUCE is ALFACE (f)   (ALFAS)
Imagine saying, "I'LL FUSS if I don't get
lettuce."

○ The Portuguese for ONION is CEBOLA   (SBOLA)
Imagine one onion saying to another, "THEY
BOIL An onion in this place."

○ The Portuguese for ASPARAGUS is
ESPARGO   (ESHPARGOO)
Imagine ASPARAGUS in Port wine.

○ The Portuguese for GRAPE is UVA   (OOVA)
Imagine saying, "YOU'VE A grape in your
mouth."

○ The Portuguese for PEAR is PERA   (PERA)
Imagine a PAIR O' pears.

○ The Portuguese for APPLE is MAÇÃ   (MASANG)
Imagine an apple is MISSING.

○ The Portuguese for WALNUT is NOZ (f)   (NOSH)
Imagine stuffing a walnut up someone's
NOSE.

○ The Portuguese for FIG is FIGO   (FEEGOO)
Imagine covering FIGS in Port wine.

YOU CAN WRITE YOUR ANSWERS IN

○ What is the English for FIGO? _____

○ What is the English for NOZ (f)? _____

○ What is the English for MAÇÃ? _____

○ What is the English for PERA? _____

○ What is the English for UVA? _____

○ What is the English for ESPARGO? _____

○ What is the English for CEBOLA? _____

○ What is the English for ALFACE (f)? _____

○ What is the English for ANCHOVA? _____

○ What is the English for ATUM? _____

TURN BACK FOR THE ANSWERS

COVER UP THE LEFT HAND PAGE BEFORE ANSWERING

○ What is the Portuguese for fig? _____

○ What is the Portuguese for walnut? _____

○ What is the Portuguese for apple? _____

○ What is the Portuguese for pear? _____

○ What is the Portuguese for grape? _____

○ What is the Portuguese for asparagus? _____

○ What is the Portuguese for onion? _____

○ What is the Portuguese for lettuce? _____

○ What is the Portuguese for anchovy? _____

○ What is the Portuguese for tunny? _____

TURN BACK FOR THE ANSWERS

SOME MORE USEFUL WORDS

THINK OF EACH IMAGE IN YOUR MIND'S EYE FOR ABOUT TEN SECONDS

○ The Portuguese for CONVENIENT is
CONVENIENTE (KONVNIENT)
Imagine drinking Port wine because it is
CONVENIENT to get.

○ The Portuguese for COOL (or FRESH) is
FRESCO (FRESHKOO)
Imagine feeling COOL and FRESH.

○ The Portuguese for DIFFICULT is DIFÍCIL (DEEFEESEEL)
Imagine finding it DIFFICULT to drink Port
wine.

○ The Portuguese for EASY is FÁCIL (FASEEL)
Imagine someone with a FACILity for taking
things EASY.

○ The Portuguese for HOT is QUENTE (KENT)
Imagine it is HOT in KENT.

○ The Portuguese for COLD is FRIO (FREE OO)
Imagine they FREE YOU when it is COLD.

○ The Portuguese for FIRST is PRIMEIRO (PREEMEIROO)
Imagine going to a film PREMIERE, the
FIRST showing of a film.

○ The Portuguese for LAST is ÚLTIMO (OOLTEEMOO)
Imagine missing the LAST train, the
ULTIMATE disaster.

○ The Portuguese for HERE is AQUI (AKEE)
Imagine A KEY is HERE.

○ The Portuguese for THERE is ALI (ALEE)
Imagine you were THERE when Mohammed
ALI won the World Boxing Crown.

YOU CAN WRITE YOUR ANSWERS IN

○ What is the English for ALI? _____

○ What is the English for AQUI? _____

○ What is the English for ÚLTIMO? _____

○ What is the English for PRIMEIRO? _____

○ What is the English for FRIO? _____

○ What is the English for QUENTE? _____

○ What is the English for FÁCIL? _____

○ What is the English for DIFÍCIL? _____

○ What is the English for FRESCO? _____

○ What is the English for CONVENIENTE? _____

TURN BACK FOR THE ANSWERS

COVER UP THE LEFT HAND PAGE BEFORE ANSWERING

O What is the Portuguese for there? _____

O What is the Portuguese for here? _____

O What is the Portuguese for last? _____

O What is the Portuguese for first? _____

O What is the Portuguese for cold? _____

O What is the Portuguese for hot? _____

O What is the Portuguese for easy? _____

O What is the Portuguese for difficult? _____

O What is the Portuguese for cool (or fresh)? _____

O What is the Portuguese for convenient? _____

TURN BACK FOR THE ANSWERS

ELEMENTARY GRAMMAR

It is very easy to say THERE IS or THERE ARE in Portuguese.

You simply say HÁ (pronounced A).

So, for example,

THERE IS A DOG IN THE HOUSE is HÁ UM CÃO NA CASA

THERE ARE TEN TOMATOES is HÁ DEZ TOMATES

Now cover up the answers below and translate the following:

(You can write your answers in)

1. O ESPARGO E UMA NOZ ESTÃO FORA DA CASA
2. É DIFÍCIL. HÁ FIGOS E UVAS ALI
3. HÁ UM ATUM E UMA ANCHOVA NO LEITE
4. AQUI, ENTRE A CASA DE BANHO E O DUCHE, HÁ UM ESPELHO
5. O ALHO ESTÁ NA MAÇÃ. É CONVENIENTE

The answers are:

1. THE ASPARAGUS AND A WALNUT ARE OUTSIDE THE HOUSE
2. IT IS DIFFICULT. THERE ARE FIGS AND GRAPES THERE
3. THERE IS A TUNNY AND AN ANCHOVY IN THE MILK
4. HERE, BETWEEN THE BATHROOM AND THE SHOWER, THERE IS A MIRROR
5. THE GARLIC IS IN (or ON) THE APPLE. IT IS CONVENIENT

Now cover up the answers below and translate the following:

(You can write your answers in)

1. THERE ARE TWENTY-FIVE COLD APPLES IN THE DRAWER
2. THERE ARE SIX FRESH (COOL) PEARS UNDER A TABLE
3. IT IS EASY. THERE IS AN ONION IN THE LETTUCE
4. IT IS CONVENIENT. THERE ARE GRAPES AND FIGS HERE
5. THE FIRST TUNNY AND THE LAST ANCHOVY ARE HOT

The answers are:

1. HÁ VINTE E CINCO MAÇÃS FRIAS NA GAVETA
2. HÁ SEIS PERAS FRESCAS DEBAIXO DUMA MESA
3. É FÁCIL. HÁ UMA CEBOLA NA ALFACE
4. É CONVENIENTE. HÁ UVAS E FIGOS AQUI
5. O PRIMEIRO ATUM E A ÚLTIMA ANCHOVA ESTÃO QUENTES

N.B. PRIMEIRO and ÚLTIMO always come *before* the word they go with.

158

Section 7 SHOPPING AND BUSINESS WORDS

SHOPPING

THINK OF EACH IMAGE IN YOUR MIND'S EYE FOR ABOUT TEN SECONDS

○ The Portuguese for MARKET is MERCADO   (MERKADOO)
  Imagine a performance of the MIKADO in the market.

○ The Portuguese for SHOP is LOJA   (LOjA)
  Imagine your LODGER owns a shop.

○ The Portuguese for SALESMAN is
  VENDEDOR   (VENDeDOR)
  Imagine a German saying, "VEN DE DOR rings, it is a salesman."

○ The Portuguese for BANK is BANCO   (BANKOO)
  Imagine placing Port wine in a BANK.

○ The Portuguese for POST OFFICE is
  CORREIO   (KOORRE YOO)
  Imagine you have a CAREER in a post office.

○ The Portuguese for MONEY is DINHEIRO   (DEENYEIROO)
  Imagine you pay money for the DINNER YOU had.

○ The Portuguese for CHEQUE is CHEQUE   (SHEK)
  Imagine paying a large CHEQUE for a special bottle of Port wine.

○ The Portuguese for PURSE is BOLSA   (BOLSA)
  Imagine a purse made of BALSA wood.

○ The Portuguese for RECEIPT is RECIBO   (ReSEEBOO)
  Imagine you spill Port wine on your RECEIPT.

○ The Portuguese for CASHIER is CAIXA (m or f)   (KAISHA)
  Imagine a KOSHER cashier.

159

YOU CAN WRITE YOUR ANSWERS IN

○ What is the English for CAIXA (m or f)? _____

○ What is the English for RECIBO? _____

○ What is the English for BOLSA? _____

○ What is the English for CHEQUE? _____

○ What is the English for DINHEIRO? _____

○ What is the English for CORREIO? _____

○ What is the English for BANCO? _____

○ What is the English for VENDEDOR? _____

○ What is the English for LOJA? _____

○ What is the English for MERCADO? _____

TURN BACK FOR THE ANSWERS

COVER UP THE LEFT HAND PAGE BEFORE ANSWERING

○ What is the Portuguese for cashier? _____

○ What is the Portuguese for receipt? _____

○ What is the Portuguese for purse? _____

○ What is the Portuguese for cheque? _____

○ What is the Portuguese for money? _____

○ What is the Portuguese for post office? _____

○ What is the Portuguese for bank? _____

○ What is the Portuguese for salesman? _____

○ What is the Portuguese for shop? _____

○ What is the Portuguese for market? _____

TURN BACK FOR THE ANSWERS

ELEMENTARY GRAMMAR

The way to ask a question in Portuguese is very easy. You normally do it by tone of voice. You do not need to change the word order in any way.

So,

IT IS A BULL	is	É UM TOURO?
IS IT A BULL?	is	É UM TOURO?
HE HAS A BULL	is	TEM UM TOURO
HAS HE (or DOES HE HAVE) A BULL?	is	TEM UM TOURO?
DO YOU EAT THE COW?	is	COME A VACA?
DOES SHE HAVE A FLOWER?	is	TEM UMA FLOR?
IS THERE A WASHBASIN?	is	HÁ UM LAVATÓRIO?

and so on.

Now cover up the answers below and translate the following:

(You can write your answers in)

1. AS LOJAS E OS BANCOS SÃO DEBAIXO DA PONTE?
2. HÁ UM MERCADO GRANDE AQUI?
3. É UM RAPAZ SUJO. COME GATOS?
4. HÁ UMA RETRETE ALI?
5. QUER UM RECIBO PEQUENO?

The answers are:

1. ARE THE SHOPS AND THE BANKS UNDER THE BRIDGE?
2. IS THERE A BIG MARKET HERE?
3. IT (HE) IS A DIRTY BOY. DOES HE EAT CATS?
4. IS THERE A TOILET THERE?*
5. DOES HE (or SHE, or DO YOU) WANT A SMALL RECEIPT?

*Another word for toilet is CASA DE BANHO (bathroom).

Now cover up the answers below and translate the following:

(You can write your answers in)

1. IS THERE A MARKET IN THE CITY?
2. IS IT CONVENIENT?
3. IS THE SALESMAN IN THE POST OFFICE?
4. HAVE YOU THE MONEY AND THE CHEQUE IN THE PURSE?
5. DOES THE CASHIER WANT A RECEIPT?

The answers are:

1. HÁ UM MERCADO NA CIDADE?
2. É CONVENIENTE?
3. O VENDEDOR ESTÁ NO CORREIO?
4. TEM O DINHEIRO E O CHEQUE NA BOLSA?
5. O CAIXA QUER UM RECIBO?

BUSINESS

THINK OF EACH IMAGE IN YOUR MIND'S EYE FOR ABOUT TEN SECONDS

○ The Portuguese for MANAGER is
GERENTE   (jeRENT)
Imagine asking for THE RENT
manager.

○ The Portuguese for OWNER is
PROPRIETÁRIO   (PROOPREE ETARYOO)
Imagine the owner, the PROPRIETOR
of a business.

○ The Portuguese for JOB is EMPREGO   (EMPREGOO)
Imagine you have a job IMPREGnating
penguins.

○ The Portuguese for FACTORY is
FÁBRICA   (FABREEKA)
Imagine a factory making FABRICS.

○ The Portuguese for TAX is IMPOSTO   (EEMPOSHTOO)
Imagine a tax is IMPOSED on you.

○ The Portuguese for BUSINESS is
NEGÓCIO   (NEGOSYOO)
Imagine you NEGOCIATE to buy a
business.

○ The Portuguese for INSURANCE is
SEGURO   (SeGOOROO)
Imagine an insurance man smoking a fat
CIGAR OH!

○ The Portuguese for LABEL is
ETIQUETA   (ETEEKETA)
Imagine it is good ETIQUETTE to put
labels on products.

○ The Portuguese for DEPARTMENT is
DEPARTAMENTO   (DEPARTAMENTOO)
Imagine a DEPARTMENT selling only
Port wine.

○ The Portuguese for BRAND is MARCA   (MARKA)
Imagine you MARK A product with its
brand name.

165

YOU CAN WRITE YOUR ANSWERS IN

○ What is the English for MARCA? _____

○ What is the English for
DEPARTAMENTO? _____

○ What is the English for ETIQUETA? _____

○ What is the English for SEGURO? _____

○ What is the English for NEGÓCIO? _____

○ What is the English for IMPOSTO? _____

○ What is the English for FÁBRICA? _____

○ What is the English for EMPREGO? _____

○ What is the English for
PROPRIETÁRIO? _____

○ What is the English for GERENTE? _____

TURN BACK FOR THE ANSWERS

YOU CAN WRITE YOUR ANSWERS IN

○ What is the Portuguese for brand?   _____

○ What is the Portuguese for department?   _____

○ What is the Portuguese for label?   _____

○ What is the Portuguese for insurance?   _____

○ What is the Portuguese for business?   _____

○ What is the Portuguese for tax?   _____

○ What is the Portuguese for factory?   _____

○ What is the Portuguese for job?   _____

○ What is the Portuguese for owner?   _____

○ What is the Portuguese for manager?   _____

TURN BACK FOR THE ANSWERS

WORDS FOR ASKING QUESTIONS

THINK OF EACH IMAGE IN YOUR MIND'S EYE FOR ABOUT TEN SECONDS

○ The Portuguese for WHERE is ONDE   (OND)
  Imagine asking, "WHERE ON THE body is
  the spine?"

○ The Portuguese for WHEN is QUANDO   (KWANDOO)
  Imagine asking WHEN you CAN DO these
  things.

○ The Portuguese for WHO is QUEM   (KENG)
  Imagine asking, "WHO killed the KING?"

○ The Portuguese for WHY is PORQUE   (POORKE)
  Imagine asking, "WHY have I got such a
  POOR KEY for opening doors?"

○ The Portuguese for HOW is COMO   (KOMOO)
  Imagine the singer Perry COMO asking HOW
  to sing.

○ The Portuguese for HOW MUCH is QUANTO   (KWANTOO)
  Imagine asking HOW MUCH it costs to fly to
  Australia with QUANTAS Airlines.

Please note: HOW MANY is QUANTO in the plural – QUANTOS

YOU CAN WRITE YOUR ANSWERS IN

○ What is the English for QUANTO? _____

○ What is the English for COMO? _____

○ What is the English for PORQUE? _____

○ What is the English for QUEM? _____

○ What is the English for QUANDO? _____

○ What is the English for ONDE? _____

TURN BACK FOR THE ANSWERS

○ What is the Portuguese for how much?   _____

○ What is the Portuguese for how?   _____

○ What is the Portuguese for why?   _____

○ What is the Portuguese for who?   _____

○ What is the Portuguese for when?   _____

○ What is the Portuguese for where?   _____

TURN BACK FOR THE ANSWERS

SHOPS

THINK OF EACH IMAGE IN YOUR MIND'S EYE FOR ABOUT TEN SECONDS

○ The Portuguese for CHEMIST'S SHOP is
FARMÁCIA   (FARMASYA)
Imagine the PHARMACY in your local
chemist's shop.

○ The Portuguese for DAIRY is LEITARIA   (LEITAREE A)
Imagine LITTER all over the dairy floor.

○ The Portuguese for LAUNDERETTE is
LAVANDARIA   (LAVANDeREE A)
Imagine your launderette smells of
LAVENDER water.

○ The Portuguese for SUPERMARKET is
SUPERMERCADO   (SOOPERMERKADOO)
Imagine a SUPERMARKET doing a
promotion of Port wine.

○ The Portuguese for BUTCHER'S SHOP is
TALHO   (TALYOO)
Imagine butchers TELL YOU to eat more
meat.

○ The Portuguese for BAKERY is PADARIA   (PADeREE A)
Imagine when your mother goes to the bakery
they PAD HER EAR with dough.

YOU CAN WRITE YOUR ANSWERS IN

○ What is the English for PADARIA? _____

○ What is the English for TALHO? _____

○ What is the English for
SUPERMERCADO? _____

○ What is the English for LAVANDARIA? _____

○ What is the English for LEITARIA? _____

○ What is the English for FARMÁCIA? _____

TURN BACK FOR THE ANSWERS

COVER UP THE LEFT HAND PAGE BEFORE ANSWERING

○ What is the Portuguese for bakery? _____

○ What is the Portuguese for butcher's shop? _____

○ What is the Portuguese for supermarket? _____

○ What is the Portuguese for launderette? _____

○ What is the Portuguese for dairy? _____

○ What is the Portuguese for chemist's shop? _____

TURN BACK FOR THE ANSWERS

ELEMENTARY GRAMMAR

When you ask questions using words like WHERE?, WHEN? or WHY? you usually do it in much the same way as in English.

The word order sometimes changes a little, but don't worry too much about this. It is not crucial in making yourself understood.

Here are some examples:

PORQUE TEM A MOSCA CINCO MESAS?
WHY DOES THE FLY HAVE FIVE TABLES?

COMO QUER OS PATOS?
HOW DOES HE (or SHE, YOU) WANT THE DUCKS?

QUEM COME A ANCHOVA?
WHO EATS THE ANCHOVY?

ONDE É O RESTAURANTE?
WHERE IS THE RESTAURANT?

QUANTO COME O INSECTO?
HOW MUCH DOES THE INSECT EAT?

QUANDO COME NUM RESTAURANTE?
WHEN DO YOU (or DOES HE, DOES SHE) EAT IN A RESTAURANT?

QUANTO is like an adjective. It becomes QUANTA or QUANTOS or QUANTAS depending on the noun it comes before.

So,

HOW MUCH WATER? is QUANTA ÁGUA?
HOW MANY TABLES? is QUANTAS MESAS?

Now cover up the answers below and translate the following:

(You can write your answers in)

1. QUANTO É O SEGURO?
2. PORQUE TEM MENOS TEMPO?
3. A LAVANDARIA, O SUPERMERCADO E O TALHO SÃO NA CIDADE?
4. É UM BOM NEGÓCIO MAS OS IMPOSTOS SÃO ALTOS
5. HÁ QUANTOS DEPARTAMENTOS NA FÁBRICA?

The answers are:

1. HOW MUCH IS THE INSURANCE?
2. WHY DO YOU (or DOES HE, DOES SHE) HAVE LESS TIME?
3. ARE THE LAUNDERETTE, THE SUPERMARKET AND THE BUTCHER'S SHOP IN THE CITY?
4. IT IS A GOOD BUSINESS BUT THE TAXES ARE HIGH
5. HOW MANY DEPARTMENTS ARE THERE IN THE FACTORY?

Now cover up the answers below and translate the following:

(You can write your answers in)

1. WHERE ARE THE CHEMIST'S SHOP, THE DAIRY AND THE BAKERY?

2. WHEN IS IT A GOOD BRAND?

3. WHO IS THE OWNER AND WHO IS THE MANAGER? WHERE IS THE FACTORY?

4. HOW AND WHEN DO YOU WANT THE LABEL?

5. HOW MANY JOBS ARE THERE?

The answers are:

1. ONDE SÃO A FARMÁCIA, A LEITARIA E A PADARIA?

2. QUANDO É UMA BOA MARCA?

3. QUEM É O PROPRIETARIO E QUEM É O GERENTE? ONDE É A FÁBRICA?

4. COMO E QUANDO QUER A ETIQUETA?

5. HÁ QUANTOS EMPREGOS?

Section 8 TRAVELLING, THE CAR

TRAVELLING

THINK OF EACH IMAGE IN YOUR MIND'S EYE FOR ABOUT TEN SECONDS

○ The Portuguese for YES is SIM   (SING)
  Imagine you SING "YES, Yes."

○ The Portuguese for NO is NÃO   (NAONG)
  Imagine NO is not a NOUN.

○ The Portuguese for PASSPORT is
  PASSAPORTE   (PASAPORT)
  Imagine a bottle of Port wine on top of your
  PASSPORT.

○ The Portuguese for CUSTOMS is
  ALFÂNDEGA   (ALFANDEGA)
  Imagine having an argument with a female
  customs officer, and you end up by
  OFFENDING HER.

○ The Portuguese for BAG is SACO   (SAKOO)
  Imagine your boss threatens to SACK YOU
  for bringing the wrong bag.

○ The Portuguese for TICKET is BILHETE   (BEELYET)
  Imagine thinking, "I'll BE LATE if you don't
  get the tickets soon."

○ The Portuguese for ENTRANCE is
  ENTRADA   (ENTRADA)
  Imagine saying, "ENTER THERE by the
  entrance."

○ The Portuguese for EXIT is SAÍDA   (SA EEDA)
  Imagine CIDER over the exit to a cinema.

○ The Portuguese for CLOSED is FECHADO   (FESHADOO)
  Imagine seeing a FAIR SHADOW over a
  place which has clearly CLOSED down.

○ The Portuguese for OPEN is ABERTO   (ABERTOO)
  Imagine a door is OPEN for you and A BEAR
  TOO, if he wants to go through.

YOU CAN WRITE YOUR ANSWERS IN

○ What is the English for ABERTO? _____

○ What is the English for FECHADO? _____

○ What is the English for SAÍDA? _____

○ What is the English for ENTRADA? _____

○ What is the English for BILHETE? _____

○ What is the English for SACO? _____

○ What is the English for ALFÂNDEGA? _____

○ What is the English for PASSAPORTE? _____

○ What is the English for NÃO? _____

○ What is the English for SIM? _____

TURN BACK FOR THE ANSWERS

COVER UP THE LEFT HAND PAGE BEFORE ANSWERING

○ What is the Portuguese for open? _____

○ What is the Portuguese for closed? _____

○ What is the Portuguese for exit? _____

○ What is the Portuguese for entrance? _____

○ What is the Portuguese for ticket? _____

○ What is the Portuguese for bag? _____

○ What is the Portuguese for customs? _____

○ What is the Portuguese for passport? _____

○ What is the Portuguese for no? _____

○ What is the Portuguese for yes? _____

TURN BACK FOR THE ANSWERS

SOME VERBS

○ The Portuguese for BUYS (or YOU BUY) is
  COMPRA   (KOMPRA)
  Imagine you should always COMPARE what
  YOU BUY with what I buy.

○ The Portuguese for SELLS (or YOU SELL) is
  VENDE   (VEND)
  Imagine YOU SELL goods to a street
  VENDOR.

○ The Portuguese for I HAVE is TENHO   (TENYOO)
  Imagine thinking, "I HAVE a TEN YEAR
  old child."

○ The Portuguese for I SEE is VEJO   (VEjOO)
  Imagine saying, "I SEE a VISION."

YOU CAN WRITE YOUR ANSWERS IN

○ What is the English for VEJO?   _____

○ What is the English for TENHO?   _____

○ What is the English for VENDE?   _____

○ What is the English for COMPRA?   _____

TURN BACK FOR THE ANSWERS

COVER UP THE LEFT HAND PAGE BEFORE ANSWERING

○ What is the Portuguese for I see? _____

○ What is the Portuguese for I have? _____

○ What is the Portuguese for sells (or you sell)? _____

○ What is the Portuguese for buys (or you buy)? _____

TURN BACK FOR THE ANSWERS

ELEMENTARY GRAMMAR

You will have noticed that you only need one word in Portuguese to say I HAVE (TENHO) or I SEE (VEJO).

It is the "O" at the end of the Portuguese word that stands for the "I" in English.

You can use this "O" with other verbs you have already learned.

For example,

    I BUY is COMPRO
    I SELL is VENDO
  I WANT is QUERO
    I EAT is COMO

Now cover up the answers below and translate the following:

(You can write your answers in)

1. VEJO A ALFÂNDEGA
2. SIM, A LOJA ESTÁ ABERTA E COMPRO UM SACO
3. TENHO SETE SAIAS LIMPAS
4. NÃO, VENDO BILHETES
5. O RESTAURANTE ESTÁ FECHADO? SIM, MAS O EDIFÍCIO ESTÁ ABERTO

The answers are:

1. I SEE THE CUSTOMS
2. YES, THE SHOP IS OPEN AND I BUY A BAG
3. I HAVE SEVEN CLEAN SKIRTS
4. NO, I SELL TICKETS
5. IS THE RESTAURANT CLOSED? YES, BUT THE BUILDING IS OPEN

Now cover up the answers below and translate the following:

(You can write your answers in)

1. SHE BUYS THE BLUE BAG
2. I BUY THE TICKET
3. THE BOY WANTS THE EXIT. I WANT THE ENTRANCE
4. I SELL PASSPORTS BUT THE SHOP IS CLOSED
5. NO, I SEE A PATH AND I WANT A GARDEN

The answers are:

1. COMPRA O SACO AZUL
2. COMPRO O BILHETE
3. O RAPAZ QUER A SAÍDA. QUERO A ENTRADA
4. VENDO PASSAPORTES MAS A LOJA ESTÁ FECHADA
5. NÃO, VEJO UM CAMINHO E QUERO UM JARDIM

VEHICLES AND TRAVELLING

THINK OF EACH IMAGE IN YOUR MIND'S EYE FOR ABOUT TEN SECONDS

○ The Portuguese for CAR is CARRO   (KARROO)
  Imagine a car filled with bottles of Port
  wine.

○ The Portuguese for BUS is
  AUTOCARRO   (A OOTOKARROO)
  Imagine an AUTOmatic CAR used as a bus.

○ The Portuguese for TAXI is TÁXI   (TAKSEE)
  Imagine a TAXI filled with bottles of Port
  wine.

○ The Portuguese for TRAIN is COMBOIO   (KOMBOYOO)
  Imagine asking if I CAN BUY YOU a train
  for Christmas.

○ The Portuguese for BOAT is BARCO   (BARKOO)
  Imagine telling a dog to BARK OH! or you'll
  throw him off the boat.

○ The Portuguese for MAP is MAPA (m)   (MAPA)
  Imagine spilling a bottle of Port wine over a
  MAP.

○ The Portuguese for STREET is RUA   (ROO A)
  Imagine you RUE A time when you slept in
  the street.

○ The Portuguese for DRIVER is CONDUTOR (KONDOOTOR)
  Imagine a bus CONDUCTOR driving your
  car.

○ The Portuguese for GARAGE is
  GARAGEM (f)   (GARAjENG)
  Imagine GARAGING your car in a garage.

○ The Portuguese for (CAR) BOOT (TRUNK) is
  MALA   (MALA)
  Imagine the composer MAHLER lying in your
  car boot.

189

YOU CAN WRITE YOUR ANSWERS IN

O What is the English for MALA?   _____

O What is the English for GARAGEM (f)?   _____

O What is the English for CONDUTOR?   _____

O What is the English for RUA?   _____

O What is the English for MAPA (m)?   _____

O What is the English for BARCO?   _____

O What is the English for COMBOIO?   _____

O What is the English for TÁXI?   _____

O What is the English for AUTOCARRO?   _____

O What is the English for CARRO?   _____

TURN BACK FOR THE ANSWERS

○ What is the Portuguese for (car) boot?   _____

○ What is the Portuguese for garage?   _____

○ What is the Portuguese for driver?   _____

○ What is the Portuguese for street?   _____

○ What is the Portuguese for map?   _____

○ What is the Portuguese for boat?   _____

○ What is the Portuguese for train?   _____

○ What is the Portuguese for taxi?   _____

○ What is the Portuguese for bus?   _____

○ What is the Portuguese for car?   _____

TURN BACK FOR THE ANSWERS

SOME MORE VEHICLE WORDS

THINK OF EACH IMAGE IN YOUR MIND'S EYE FOR ABOUT TEN SECONDS

○ The Portuguese for PETROL is GASOLINA (GAZOOLEENA)
Imagine an American petrol station with its
GASOLINE sign on the forecourt.

○ The Portuguese for OIL is ÓLEO (OLYOO)
Imagine shouting "OLE!" as you pour oil in
your car.

○ The Portuguese for PUNCTURE is FURO (FOOROO)
Imagine being FURIOUS after you get a
puncture.

○ The Portuguese for BREAKDOWN is
AVARIA (AVAREE A)
Imagine hearing a choir singing "AVE
MARIA" after you have broken down.

○ The Portuguese for BATTERY is BATERIA (BATeREE A)
Imagine pouring bottles of Port wine into a
BATTERY.

○ The Portuguese for EXHAUST is TUBO DE
ESCAPE (TOOBOO DESHKAP)
Imagine fitting a TUBE to ESCAPE from
exhaust fumes.

○ The Portuguese for WHEEL is RODA (RODA)
Imagine using a wheel as a RUDDER in a
small boat.

○ The Portuguese for PUMP is BOMBA (BOMBA)
Imagine someone placing a BOMB on your
pump so that it blows up when you start to
pump fuel.

○ The Portuguese for RADIATOR is
RADIADOR (RADYADOR)
Imagine pouring bottles of Port wine into your
RADIATOR.

○ The Portuguese for STEERING WHEEL is
VOLANTE (VOOLANT)
Imagine turning your steering wheel
VIOLENTLY.

193

YOU CAN WRITE YOUR ANSWERS IN

○ What is the English for VOLANTE? _____

○ What is the English for RADIADOR? _____

○ What is the English for BOMBA? _____

○ What is the English for RODA? _____

○ What is the English for TUBO DE ESCAPE? _____

○ What is the English for BATERIA? _____

○ What is the English for AVARIA? _____

○ What is the English for FURO? _____

○ What is the English for ÓLEO? _____

○ What is the English for GASOLINA? _____

TURN BACK FOR THE ANSWERS

○ What is the Portuguese for steering wheel? _____

○ What is the Portuguese for radiator? _____

○ What is the Portuguese for pump? _____

○ What is the Portuguese for wheel? _____

○ What is the Portuguese for exhaust? _____

○ What is the Portuguese for battery? _____

○ What is the Portuguese for breakdown? _____

○ What is the Portuguese for puncture? _____

○ What is the Portuguese for oil? _____

○ What is the Portuguese for petrol? _____

TURN BACK FOR THE ANSWERS

ELEMENTARY GRAMMAR

To use the word "not" in Portuguese, you put NÃO in front of the verb.

So,

THE FLY DOES NOT EAT is, literally, "The fly not eats"
which in Portuguese is, A MOSCA NÃO COME

IT IS THE BULL is, É O TOURO

IT IS NOT THE BULL is, NÃO É O TOURO

THERE ARE SEVEN
ICE CREAMS is, HÁ SETE GELADOS

THERE ARE NOT SEVEN
ICE CREAMS is, NÃO HÁ SETE GELADOS

Now cover up the answers below and translate the following:

(You can write your answers in)

1. SIM, HÁ UM FURO MAS A RODA NÃO É VELHA

2. NÃO TENHO A BOMBA MAS VEJO O TUBO DE ESCAPE E A MALA

3. NÃO É UM BARCO, É UM CARRO

4. O CONDUTOR NÃO ESTÁ FORA DA GARAGEM

5. NÃO, NÃO VENDO RODAS, MAS VENDO MAPAS E VOLANTES

The answers are:

1. YES, THERE IS A PUNCTURE BUT THE WHEEL IS NOT OLD

2. I DO NOT HAVE THE PUMP BUT I SEE THE EXHAUST AND THE BOOT

3. IT IS NOT A BOAT, IT IS A CAR

4. THE DRIVER IS NOT OUTSIDE THE GARAGE

5. NO, I DO NOT SELL WHEELS, BUT I SELL MAPS AND STEERING WHEELS

Now cover up the answers below and translate the following:

(You can write your answers in)

1. NO, I DO NOT BUY THE MAP
2. THE CAR AND THE BUS ARE NOT IN THE GARAGE AND I DO NOT HAVE THE BATTERY
3. IT IS NOT A BREAKDOWN, BUT THE TRAIN IS IN THE STREET
4. THE TAXI AND THE BOAT ARE NOT HERE BUT THE DRIVER IS FREE
5. THE PETROL AND THE OIL ARE NOT IN THE RADIATOR

The answers are:

1. NÃO, NÃO COMPRO O MAPA
2. O CARRO E O AUTOCARRO NÃO ESTÃO NA GARAGEM E NÃO TENHO A BATERIA
3. NÃO É UMA AVARIA MAS O COMBOIO ESTÁ NA RUA
4. O TÁXI E O BARCO NÃO ESTÃO AQUI MAS O CONDUTOR ESTÁ LIVRE
5. A GASOLINA E O ÓLEO NÃO ESTÃO NO RADIADOR

Section 9   ON THE BEACH AND LEISURE

THINK OF EACH IMAGE IN YOUR MIND'S EYE FOR ABOUT TEN SECONDS

○ The Portuguese for BEACH is PRAIA   (PRA YA)
  Imagine trying to PRY A tin open
  when you are sitting on the beach.

○ The Portuguese for SAND is AREIA   (AREIA)
  Imagine A RAY O' sunlight shining on
  the sand.

○ The Portuguese for DANGEROUS is
  PERIGOSO   (PEREEGOZOO)
  Imagine champagne PERRY GOES
  OOH! when it is dangerous to drink.

○ The Portuguese for SUN is SOL   (SOL)
  Imagine King SAUL, in the Bible
  story, staring up at the sun.

○ The Portuguese for SWIMMER is
  BANHISTA (m or f)   (BANYEESTA)
  Imagine a swimmer sliding down a
  BANNISTER.

○ The Portuguese for PICNIC is
  PIQUENIQUE   (PEEKNEEK)
  Imagine a PICNIC at which you drink
  only Port wine.

○ The Portuguese for TOWEL is
  TOALHA   (TOALYA)
  Imagine saying to your friend, "I will
  TOWEL YA down with this towel."

○ The Portuguese for SEA is MAR   (MAR)
  Imagine shouting, "MA, get out of the
  sea before you drown!"

○ The Portuguese for DECKCHAIR
  is CADAIRA DE REPOUSO (f)   (KADEIRA De RePOZOO)
  Imagine a deckchair to REPOSE YOU

○ The Portuguese for WAVE is ONDA   (ONDA)
  Imagine a wave ON THE beach.

YOU CAN WRITE YOUR ANSWERS IN

○ What is the English for ONDA? _____

○ What is the English for CADEIRA DE REPOUSO (f)? _____

○ What is the English for MAR? _____

○ What is the English for TOALHA? _____

○ What is the English for PIQUENIQUE? _____

○ What is the English for BANHISTA (m or f)? _____

○ What is the English for SOL? _____

○ What is the English for PERIGOSO? _____

○ What is the English for AREIA? _____

○ What is the English for PRAIA? _____

TURN BACK FOR THE ANSWERS

○ What is the Portuguese for wave?   _____

○ What is the Portuguese for deckchair?   _____

○ What is the Portuguese for sea?   _____

○ What is the Portuguese for towel?   _____

○ What is the Portuguese for picnic?   _____

○ What is the Portuguese for swimmer?   _____

○ What is the Portuguese for sun?   _____

○ What is the Portuguese for dangerous? _____

○ What is the Portuguese for sand?   _____

○ What is the Portuguese for beach?   _____

TURN BACK FOR THE ANSWERS

SOME MORE LEISURE WORDS

THINK OF EACH IMAGE IN YOUR MIND'S EYE FOR ABOUT TEN SECONDS

○ The Portuguese for EXCURSION is
EXCURSÃO (f)   (ESHKOORSAONG)
Imagine taking plenty of bottles of Port wine
with you on an EXCURSION to the
countryside.

○ The Portuguese for RIVER is RIO   (REE OO)
Imagine a big river, the RIO Grande.

○ The Portuguese for MOUNTAIN is
MONTANHA   (MONTANYA)
Imagine the American state of MONTANA,
with big mountains.

○ The Portuguese for LAKE is LAGO   (LAGOO)
Imagine a lake full of LAGER beer.

○ The Portuguese for FOREST is FLORESTA   (FLOORESHTA)
Imagine a FLORIST selling flowers at the
edge of a forest.

○ The Portuguese for NEWSPAPER is
JORNAL   (jOORNAL)
Imagine a JOURNALIST writing for a
newspaper.

○ The Portuguese for BOOK is LIVRO   (LEEVROO)
Imagine that you LEAVE ROOM for your
books.

○ The Portuguese for LETTER is CARTA   (KARTA)
Imagine ex-President Jimmy CARTER
reading a letter.

○ The Portuguese for STAMP is SELO   (SELOO)
Imagine I SELL YOU a stamp.

○ The Portuguese for PARTY is FESTA   (FESHTA)
Imagine a huge FEAST At a party.

YOU CAN WRITE YOUR ANSWERS IN

○ What is the English for FESTA? _____

○ What is the English for SELO? _____

○ What is the English for CARTA? _____

○ What is the English for LIVRO? _____

○ What is the English for JORNAL? _____

○ What is the English for FLORESTA? _____

○ What is the English for LAGO? _____

○ What is the English for MONTANHA? _____

○ What is the English for RIO? _____

○ What is the English for EXCURSÃO (f)? _____

TURN BACK FOR THE ANSWERS

COVER UP THE LEFT HAND PAGE BEFORE ANSWERING

○ What is the Portuguese for party? _____

○ What is the Portuguese for stamp? _____

○ What is the Portuguese for letter? _____

○ What is the Portuguese for book? _____

○ What is the Portuguese for newspaper? _____

○ What is the Portuguese for forest? _____

○ What is the Portuguese for lake? _____

○ What is the Portuguese for mountain? _____

○ What is the Portuguese for river? _____

○ What is the Portuguese for excursion? _____

TURN BACK FOR THE ANSWERS

ELEMENTARY GRAMMAR

When we want to show possession in English, we say things like "the manager's department" or "the boys' meat".

In Portuguese you must always turn this round to become "the department of the manager", or "the meat of the boys".

OF, in Portuguese, is DE (pronounced De). You have met this word before in words like DEBAIXO DE, and you already know that when it comes before the Portuguese words for "the" and "a", it loses its "E" and merges with them.

So,

THE MANAGER'S DEPARTMENT is DEPARTAMENTO DO GERENTE

THE BOYS' MEAT is A CARNE DOS RAPAZES

and so on.

Now cover up the answers below and translate the following:

(You can write your answers in)

1. HÁ UMA EXCURSÃO? NÃO, MAS A FESTA DO COELHO É SEMPRE BOA

2. ONDE ESTÁ A AREIA E ONDE ESTÃO AS ONDAS? NA PRAIA

3. O SOL ESTÁ QUENTE E VEJO O PIQUENIQUE DOS BEBÉS

4. A GARRAFA DA RAPARIGA ESTÁ VAZIA

5. A PORTA DA CASA DE BANHO É AZUL

The answers are:

1. IS THERE AN EXCURSION? NO, BUT THE RABBIT'S PARTY IS ALWAYS GOOD

2. WHERE IS THE SAND AND WHERE ARE THE WAVES? ON THE BEACH

3. THE SUN IS HOT AND I SEE THE BABIES' PICNIC

4. THE GIRL'S BOTTLE IS EMPTY

5. THE DOOR OF THE BATHROOM IS BLUE

Now cover up the answers below and translate the following:

(You can write your answers in)

1. I SELL THE BOY'S NEWSPAPER
2. THE SEA IS DANGEROUS BUT THE SWIMMER'S TOWEL IS CLEAN
3. HE BUYS BOOKS, STAMPS AND LETTERS
4. I WANT THE MOTHER'S DECKCHAIR
5. IN THE FOREST THERE IS A RIVER, A MOUNTAIN AND A LAKE

The answers are:

1. VENDO O JORNAL DO RAPAZ
2. O MAR É PERIGOSO MAS A TOALHA DO (or DA) BANHISTA ESTÁ LIMPA
3. COMPRA LIVROS, SELOS E CARTAS
4. QUERO A CADEIRA DE REPOUSO DA MÃE
5. NA FLORESTA HÁ UM RIO, UMA MONTANHA E UM LAGO

SOME MORE LEISURE WORDS

THINK OF EACH IMAGE IN YOUR MIND'S EYE FOR ABOUT TEN SECONDS

○ The Portuguese for DISCO is
DISCOTECA   (DEESHKOOTEKA)
Imagine taking a bottle of Port wine to a
DISCO.

○ The Portuguese for DANCE is DANÇA   (DANSA)
Imagine seeing a DANCE through a haze of
Port wine.

○ The Portuguese for CONCERT is
CONCERTO   (KONSERTOO)
Imagine everyone at a CONCERT drinking
bottles of Port wine.

○ The Portuguese for CASTLE is CASTELO   (KASHTELOO)
Imagine Abbot and COSTELLO in a castle.

○ The Portuguese for MUSEUM is MUSEU   (MOO ZE OO)
Imagine a MUSEUM exhibiting old bottles of
Port wine.

○ The Portuguese for CINEMA is CINEMA (m)   (SEENEMA)
Imagine a CINEMA exhibiting bottles of Port
wine in the foyer.

○ The Portuguese for BULLFIGHT is
TOURADA   (TOORADA)
Imagine a TOREADOR in a bullfight.

○ The Portuguese for (A) WALK is (UM)
PASSEIO   (PAS EYOO)
Imagine PASSING YOU on a walk.

○ The Portuguese for PALACE is PALÁCIO   (PALASYOO)
Imagine a PALACE with bottles of Port wine
in the courtyard.

○ The Portuguese for CATHEDRAL is
CATEDRAL (f)   (KATeDRAL)
Imagine a CATHEDRAL with bottles of Port
wine rolling on the floor.

YOU CAN WRITE YOUR ANSWERS IN

○ What is the English for CATEDRAL (f)? _____

○ What is the English for PALÁCIO? _____

○ What is the English for (UM) PASSEIO? _____

○ What is the English for TOURADA? _____

○ What is the English for CINEMA (m)? _____

○ What is the English for MUSEU? _____

○ What is the English for CASTELO? _____

○ What is the English for CONCERTO? _____

○ What is the English for DANÇA? _____

○ What is the English for DISCOTECA? _____

TURN BACK FOR THE ANSWERS

COVER UP THE LEFT HAND PAGE BEFORE ANSWERING

○ What is the Portuguese for cathedral? _____

○ What is the Portuguese for palace? _____

○ What is the Portuguese for (a) walk? _____

○ What is the Portuguese for bullfight? _____

○ What is the Portuguese for cinema? _____

○ What is the Portuguese for museum? _____

○ What is the Portuguese for castle? _____

○ What is the Portuguese for concert? _____

○ What is the Portuguese for dance? _____

○ What is the Portuguese for disco? _____

TURN BACK FOR THE ANSWERS

ELEMENTARY GRAMMAR

To say I AM in Portuguese, you say SOU (pronounced SO) for a permanent state, and ESTOU (pronounced ESHTO) for a temporary state.

So,

    I AM TIRED is ESTOU CANSADO

    (or CANSADA if a woman is speaking)

    I AM A BOY is SOU UM RAPAZ

Now cover up the answers below and translate the following:

(You can write your answers in)

1. HÁ UMA TOURADA NO PALÁCIO MAS O CINEMA ESTÁ FECHADO

2. NÃO SOU O GERENTE. OS GERENTES ESTÃO DEBAIXO DO ARMÁRIO

3. NÃO HÁ DISCOTECA NA CIDADE MAS HÁ NOVE CASTELOS

4. ÀS QUATRO E MEIA VEJO UMA DANÇA NO RESTAURANTE E AGORA NÃO ESTOU CANSADO

5. NÃO SOU O FILHO DO CAIXA. SOU A FILHA DO VENDEDOR

The answers are:

1. THERE IS A BULLFIGHT IN THE PALACE BUT THE CINEMA IS CLOSED

2. I AM NOT THE MANAGER. THE MANAGERS ARE UNDER THE CUPBOARD

3. THERE IS NOT A DISCO (or THERE IS NO DISCO) IN THE TOWN BUT THERE ARE NINE CASTLES

4. AT HALF PAST FOUR I SEE A DANCE IN THE RESTAURANT AND NOW I AM NOT TIRED

5. I AM NOT THE CASHIER'S SON. I AM THE SALESMAN'S DAUGHTER

Now cover up the answers below and translate the following:

(You can write your answers in)

1. ON THURSDAYS THERE IS A CONCERT IN THE CASTLE
2. I AM NOT OUTSIDE THE MUSEUM, I AM IN THE CATHEDRAL
3. I AM OLD AND UGLY BUT TODAY I AM FREE
4. IS HE THERE? NO, HE IS HERE
5. IT IS AN EXCELLENT WALK

The answers are:

1. ÀS QUINTAS HÁ UM CONCERTO NO CASTELO
2. NÃO ESTOU FORA DO MUSEU, ESTOU NA CATEDRAL
3. SOU VELHO E FEIO MAS HOJE ESTOU LIVRE

   N.B. A woman would say VELHA and FEIA
4. ESTÁ ALI? NÃO, ESTÁ AQUI
5. É UM PASSEIO EXCELENTE

Section 10 EMERGENCY WORDS, THE BODY, MONTHS OF THE YEAR

EMERGENCY WORDS

THINK OF EACH IMAGE IN YOUR MIND'S EYE FOR ABOUT TEN SECONDS

○ The Portuguese for ACCIDENT is
ACIDENTE   (ASEEDENT)
Imagine having an ACCIDENT by tripping
over bottles of Port wine.

○ The Portuguese for FIRE is FOGO   (FOGOO)
Imagine seeing a fire blazing on a very
FOGGY night.

○ The Portuguese for AMBULANCE is
AMBULÂNCIA   (AMBOOLANSYA)
Imagine an AMBULANCE full of bottles of
Port wine.

○ The Portuguese for TELEPHONE is
TELEFONE   (TeLFON)
Imagine a TELEPHONE in the shape of a
bottle of Port wine.

○ The Portuguese for PAIN is DOR (f)   (DOR)
Imagine feeling a terrible pain when a DOOR
falls on you.

○ The Portuguese for ILL is DOENTE   (DOO ENT)
Imagine you DON'T like being ILL.

○ The Portuguese for THANK YOU is
OBRIGADO   (OBREEGADOO)
Imagine saying, "OH BRING HER, DO and
THANK YOU for doing so."
(N.B. If you are a woman you would say
OBRIGADA.)

○ The Portuguese for PLEASE is POR FAVOR (POOR FAVOR)
Imagine saying, "PLEASE do me a POOR
FAVOUR."

○ The Portuguese for GOODBYE is ADEUS   (AD E OOSH)
Imagine you can ADDUCE that Portuguese
people say GOODBYE when they say
ADEUS.

○ The Portuguese for HELLO is OLÁ   (OLA)
Imagine thinking, "ALL I said was HELLO."

YOU CAN WRITE YOUR ANSWERS IN

○ What is the English for OLÁ? _____

○ What is the English for ADEUS? _____

○ What is the English for POR FAVOR? _____

○ What is the English for OBRIGADO
(OBRIGADA)? _____

○ What is the English for DOENTE? _____

○ What is the English for DOR (f)? _____

○ What is the English for TELEFONE? _____

○ What is the English for AMBULÂNCIA? _____

○ What is the English for FOGO? _____

○ What is the English for ACIDENTE? _____

TURN BACK FOR THE ANSWERS

COVER UP THE LEFT HAND PAGE BEFORE ANSWERING

○ What is the Portuguese for hello? _____

○ What is the Portuguese for goodbye? _____

○ What is the Portuguese for please? _____

○ What is the Portuguese for thank you? _____

○ What is the Portuguese for ill? _____

○ What is the Portuguese for pain? _____

○ What is the Portuguese for telephone? _____

○ What is the Portuguese for ambulance? _____

○ What is the Portuguese for fire? _____

○ What is the Portuguese for accident? _____

TURN BACK FOR THE ANSWERS

THE BODY

THINK OF EACH IMAGE IN YOUR MIND'S EYE FOR ABOUT TEN SECONDS

○ The Portuguese for COUGH is TOSSE (f)   (TOS)
Imagine you TOSS a coin when you start to
cough badly.

○ The Portuguese for ANKLE is
TORNOZELO   (TOORNOOZELOO)
Imagine you TOUR NEW ZEALAND with a
bad ankle.

○ The Portuguese for BLOOD is SANGUE   (SANG)
Imagine someone SANG "Blood, blood,
glorious blood".

○ The Portuguese for BREAST is SEIO   (SE YOO)
Imagine you SAY "OOH" when you feel a
pain in your breast.

○ The Portuguese for EAR is OUVIDO   (OVEEDOO)
Imagine a German telling the painter Van
Gogh, "O VE DO like to keep our ear on."

○ The Portuguese for EYE is OLHO   (OLYOO)
Imagine telling someone with a sore eye, "I'll
OIL YOUR eye."

○ The Portuguese for FOOT is PÉ   (PE)
Imagine being told you will have to PAY to
have your foot back.

○ The Portuguese for FINGER is DEDO   (DEDOO)
Imagine asking if people in Portugal use their
fingers to eat, and being told, "Yes, THEY
DO."

○ The Portuguese for HAND is MÃO (f)   (MAONG)
Imagine being told that if you MOAN any
more you'll get a hand across you.

○ The Portuguese for MOUTH is BOCA   (BOKA)
Imagine sticking a POKER in someone's
mouth.

219

YOU CAN WRITE YOUR ANSWERS IN

○ What is the English for BOCA? _____

○ What is the English for MÃO (f)? _____

○ What is the English for DEDO? _____

○ What is the English for PÉ? _____

○ What is the English for OLHO? _____

○ What is the English for OUVIDO? _____

○ What is the English for SEIO? _____

○ What is the English for SANGUE? _____

○ What is the English for TORNOZELO? _____

○ What is the English for TOSSE (f)? _____

TURN BACK FOR THE ANSWERS

COVER UP THE LEFT HAND PAGE BEFORE ANSWERING

○ What is the Portuguese for mouth? _____

○ What is the Portuguese for hand? _____

○ What is the Portuguese for finger? _____

○ What is the Portuguese for foot? _____

○ What is the Portuguese for eye? _____

○ What is the Portuguese for ear? _____

○ What is the Portuguese for breast? _____

○ What is the Portuguese for blood? _____

○ What is the Portuguese for ankle? _____

○ What is the Portuguese for cough? _____

TURN BACK FOR THE ANSWERS

ELEMENTARY GRAMMAR

MORE ON POSSESSION
To say "my" in Portuguese, as in MY EAR or MY COUGH, you
say literally THE MY EAR, THE MY COUGH, etc.

The word for MY changes, depending on the word it goes with:

> MY in the MASCULINE is MEU (ME OO)
>
> Imagine a cat asking, "Have you got MY MEE OW!"

So,

> MY EAR is O MEU OUVIDO (the my ear)

> MY in the FEMININE is MINHA (MEENYA)
>
> Imagine saying, "Do you MEAN YA want MY cough?"

So,

> MY COUGH is A MINHA TOSSE

In the PLURAL, you add an "s" (pronounced SH) as usual.

So,

> MY BROTHERS is OS MEUS IRMÃOS
>
> MY SISTERS   is AS MINHAS IRMÃS

Now cover up the answers below and translate the following:

(You can write your answers in)

1. ADEUS. NÃO TENHO COLHER E A MINHA CHÁVENA ESTÁ VAZIA
2. A MÃO, O PÉ E O TORNOZELO ESTÃO NO FOGO
3. TENHO UMA DOR NO SEIO, AQUI
4. PORQUE TENHO TOSSE? OS MEUS FILHOS E AS MINHAS FILHAS SÃO FEIOS
5. É PERIGOSO QUANDO OS MEUS CAVALOS NÃO ESTÃO CANSADOS

The answers are:

1. GOODBYE. I DO NOT HAVE A SPOON AND MY CUP IS EMPTY
2. THE HAND, THE FOOT AND THE ANKLE ARE IN THE FIRE
3. I HAVE A PAIN IN THE BREAST, HERE
4. WHY DO I HAVE A COUGH? MY SONS AND MY DAUGHTERS ARE UGLY
5. IT IS DANGEROUS WHEN MY HORSES ARE NOT TIRED

Please note: in the sentence PORQUE TENHO TOSSE? (Why do I have a cough?), you miss out the word for "a".

223

Now cover up the answers below and translate the following:

(You can write your answers in)

1. THANK YOU. I AM ILL AND MY TELEPHONE IS IN
   THE KITCHEN

2. THE BLOOD IS IN THE EYE, IN THE EAR AND IN THE
   MOUTH. WHERE IS THE AMBULANCE?

3. IT IS AN ACCIDENT. MY RED FLOWERS ARE UNDER
   THE CAR

4. DO I HAVE A PAIN? YES ALWAYS ON MONDAYS AT
   FOUR O'CLOCK

5. HELLO, DO YOU WANT MY FINGER? YES, PLEASE

The answers are:

1. OBRIGADO (A). ESTOU DOENTE E O TELEFONE É NA
   COZINHA

2. O SANGUE ESTÁ NO OLHO, NO OUVIDO E NA BOCA.
   ONDE ESTÁ A AMBULÂNCIA?

3. É UM ACIDENTE. AS MINHAS FLORES VERMELHAS
   ESTÃO DEBAIXO DO CARRO

4. TENHO UMA DOR? SIM, SEMPRE ÀS SEGUNDAS
   ÀS QUATRO

5. OLÁ, QUER O MEU DEDO? SIM, POR FAVOR

SOME USEFUL WORDS

THINK OF EACH IMAGE IN YOUR MIND'S EYE FOR ABOUT TEN SECONDS

○ The Portuguese for DOCTOR is MÉDICO (MEDEEKOO)
Imagine asking for a MEDICAL treatment from a doctor.

○ The Portuguese for DENTIST is DENTISTA (m or f) (DENTEESHTA)
Imagine a DENTIST drinking a bottle of Port wine.

○ The Portuguese for POLICE is POLÍCIA (POOLEESYA)
Imagine the POLICE drinking bottles of Port wine.
(N.B. POLÍCIA also means POLICEMAN – it is then masculine.)

○ The Portuguese for BOARDING HOUSE is PENSÃO (f) (PENSAONG)
Imagine having to spend your PENSION to live in a boarding house.

○ The Portuguese for HOSPITAL is HOSPITAL (OSHPEETAL)
Imagine bottles of Port wine lying at the entrance to a HOSPITAL.

○ The Portuguese for EMBASSY is EMBAIXADA (EMBAISHADA)
Imagine asking for the AMBASSADOR at the US Embassy.

○ The Portuguese for FARM is QUINTA (KEENTA)
Imagine being KEEN TO see a farm.

○ The Portuguese for FRONTIER is FRONTEIRA (FRONTEIRA)
Imagine the FRONTIER littered with bottles of Port wine.

○ The Portuguese for GENTLEMEN is SENHORES (SENYORSH)
Imagine SENIOR gentlemen going to the gentlemen's toilet.

○ The Portuguese for LADIES is SENHORAS (SENYOResH)
Imagine SENIOR ladies going to the ladies' toilet.

225

YOU CAN WRITE YOUR ANSWERS IN

○ What is the English for SENHORAS? _____

○ What is the English for SENHORES? _____

○ What is the English for FRONTEIRA? _____

○ What is the English for QUINTA? _____

○ What is the English for EMBAIXADA? _____

○ What is the English for HOSPITAL? _____

○ What is the English for PENSÃO (f)? _____

○ What is the English for POLÍCIA? _____

○ What is the English for DENTISTA (m or f)? _____

○ What is the English for MÉDICO? _____

TURN BACK FOR THE ANSWERS

COVER UP THE LEFT HAND PAGE BEFORE ANSWERING

○ What is the Portuguese for ladies? _____

○ What is the Portuguese for gentlemen? _____

○ What is the Portuguese for frontier? _____

○ What is the Portuguese for farm? _____

○ What is the Portuguese for embassy? _____

○ What is the Portuguese for hospital? _____

○ What is the Portuguese for boarding house? _____

○ What is the Portuguese for police? _____

○ What is the Portuguese for dentist? _____

○ What is the Portuguese for doctor? _____

TURN BACK FOR THE ANSWERS

SOME GENERAL WORDS

THINK OF EACH IMAGE IN YOUR MIND'S EYE FOR ABOUT TEN SECONDS

○ The Portuguese for YACHT is IATE   (YAT)
  Imagine your YACHT filled with Port wine.

○ The Portuguese for WOOD (timber) is
  MADEIRA   (MADEIRA)
  Imagine pouring MADEIRA wine over a pile
  of wood.

○ The Portuguese for WATERFALL is
  CASCATA   (KeSHKATA)
  Imagine a waterfall CASCADING down.

○ The Portuguese for VILLAGE is ALDEIA   (ALDE YA)
  Imagine spending ALL DAY in a small
  village.

○ The Portuguese for PERFUME is PERFUME   (PERFOOM)
  Imagine PERFUME which smells of Port
  wine.

○ The Portuguese for PARK is PARQUE   (PARK)
  Imagine bottles of Port wine lying all over the
  PARK.

○ The Portuguese for MESSAGE is RECADO   (ReKADOO)
  Imagine you RECORD a message.

○ The Portuguese for MATCH (matchstick) is
  FÓSFORO   (FOSHFOOROO)
  Imagine a match is made of PHOSPHORUS.

○ The Portuguese for ROPE is CORDA   (KORDA)
  Imagine a CORD, a piece of rope.

○ The Portuguese for SUPPER is CEIA   (SE YA)
  Imagine a doctor telling you, "SAY AH and
  I'll give you supper."

YOU CAN WRITE YOUR ANSWERS IN

○ What is the English for CEIA? _____

○ What is the English for CORDA? _____

○ What is the English for FÓSFORO? _____

○ What is the English for RECADO? _____

○ What is the English for PARQUE? _____

○ What is the English for PERFUME? _____

○ What is the English for ALDEIA? _____

○ What is the English for CASCATA? _____

○ What is the English for MADEIRA? _____

○ What is the English for IATE? _____

TURN BACK FOR THE ANSWERS

COVER UP THE LEFT HAND PAGE BEFORE ANSWERING

○ What is the Portuguese for supper? _____

○ What is the Portuguese for rope? _____

○ What is the Portuguese for match? _____

○ What is the Portuguese for message? _____

○ What is the Portuguese for park? _____

○ What is the Portuguese for perfume? _____

○ What is the Portuguese for village? _____

○ What is the Portuguese for waterfall? _____

○ What is the Portuguese for wood (timber)? _____

○ What is the Portuguese for yacht? _____

TURN BACK FOR THE ANSWERS

231

ELEMENTARY GRAMMAR

MORE ON POSSESSION

HIS, HER, ITS, THEIR and YOUR are all said in the same way in Portuguese.

But, just like the words for MY, they change depending on the word they go with:

HIS, HER, ITS and YOUR are all SEU (pronounced SE OO) in front of a MASCULINE word, and SUA (pronounced SOO A) in front of a FEMININE word.

They become SEUS and SUAS if the word is also PLURAL.

As with the word "my", you also have to use the word for "the" in front of them: O SEU, OS SEUS, etc.

The problem with using these words is that BOTH "his" and "her" are SEU(S) in the masculine and SUA(S) in the feminine.

So,

> HIS INSECT is O SEU INSECTO
>
> HIS FLY is A SUA MOSCA

But,

> HER INSECT is exactly the same as "his insect": O SEU INSECTO
>
> HER FLY is exactly the same as "her fly": A SUA MOSCA

This is all very tricky, and you will make mistakes. Don't worry. Everybody does.

> YOUR INSECT is O SEU INSECTO
>
> YOUR FLY is A SUA MOSCA
>
> THEIR INSECTS is OS SEUS INSECTOS
>
> THEIR FLIES is AS SUAS MOSCAS

In summary:

> HIS is O SEU, A SUA, OS SEUS or AS SUAS
>
> HER is the same as "his"
>
> ITS is the same
>
> YOUR is the same
>
> THEIR is the same

Once again, do not worry if you don't get this right just now. You will pick up the idea eventually.

Now cover up the answers below and translate the following:

Please note that HE, SHE, IT and YOU, and HIS, HER, ITS, YOUR and THEIR may be interchangeable, though only one form is given in the answers. Use whichever one seems to make the most sense to you.

(You can write your answers in)

1. A CASCATA É NO MEU PARQUE
2. TEM UM FÓSFORO? NÃO, ESTOU NO HOSPITAL
3. O SEU MÉDICO E O SEU DENTISTA SÃO VELHOS
4. O POLICIA ESTÁ DEBAIXO DA SUA CASA
5. OS SENHORES E AS SENHORAS ESTÃO NOS SEUS RESTAURANTES

The answers are:

1. THE WATERFALL IS IN MY PARK
2. DO YOU HAVE A MATCH? NO, I AM IN THE HOSPITAL
3. HER DOCTOR AND HER DENTIST ARE OLD
4. THE POLICEMAN IS UNDER YOUR HOUSE
5. THE GENTLEMEN AND THE LADIES ARE IN THEIR RESTAURANTS

Now cover up the answers below and translate the following:

(You can write your answers in)

1. HIS YACHT IS BLUE AND HER PERFUME IS GREEN
2. HIS WOOD IS RED AND HER ROPE IS BLACK
3. YOUR MESSAGE IS OUTSIDE THE EMBASSY
4. HIS FARM IS THE FRONTIER
5. THE BOARDING HOUSE IS IN HER VILLAGE

The answers are:

1. O SEU IATE É AZUL E O SEU PERFUME É VERDE
2. A SUA MADEIRA É VERMELHA E A SUA CORDA É PRETA
3. O SEU RECADO ESTÁ FORA DA EMBAIXADA
4. A SUA QUINTA É A FRONTEIRA
5. A PENSÃO É NA SUA ALDEIA

MONTHS OF THE YEAR

The months of the year in Portuguese sound a little like their English equivalents, so no images will be given.

English	Portuguese	Pronounced
JANUARY	JANEIRO	(jeNEIROO)
FEBRUARY	FEVEREIRO	(FEVREIROO)
MARCH	MARÇO	(MARSOO)
APRIL	ABRIL	(ABREEL)
MAY	MAIO	(MA YOO)
JUNE	JUNHO	(jOONYOO)
JULY	JULHO	(jOOLYOO)
AUGUST	AGOSTO	(AGOSHTOO)
SEPTEMBER	SETEMBRO	(SETENGBROO)
OCTOBER	OUTUBRO	(OTOOBROO)
NOVEMBER	NOVEMBRO	(NOVENGBROO)
DECEMBER	DEZEMBRO	(DEZENGBROO)

To say IN JANUARY, etc., you say EM JANEIRO, and so on.

Now cover up the answers below and translate the following:

Please note that once again, HIS, HER, YOUR, etc., can be interchanged in the answers.

(You can write your answers in)

1. NÃO TENHO QUINTA MAS ÀS TERÇAS COMO NUM RESTAURANTE
2. A CEIA ESTÁ SEMPRE QUENTE MAS EM MARÇO A ÁGUA ESTÁ FRIA
3. O MEU CHAPÉU ESTÁ NO SEU BARCO
4. É SETEMBRO E AS LAGOSTAS SÃO PEQUENAS
5. EM OUTUBRO O SEU IATE ESTÁ VAZIO

The answers are:

1. I DO NOT HAVE A FARM BUT ON TUESDAYS I EAT IN A RESTAURANT
2. THE SUPPER IS ALWAYS HOT BUT IN MARCH THE WATER IS COLD
3. MY HAT IS IN (or ON) YOUR BOAT
4. IT IS SEPTEMBER AND THE LOBSTERS ARE SMALL
5. IN OCTOBER HER YACHT IS EMPTY

Now cover up the answers below and translate the following:

(You can write your answers in)

1. I SELL BOATS IN JANUARY, IN MARCH, IN APRIL, IN JUNE AND IN JULY

2. MY MILK IS COLD IN NOVEMBER AND IN DECEMBER

3. THERE ARE FOUR SUNDAYS IN AUGUST

4. I EAT HIS DUCKS IN FEBRUARY AND HIS COWS IN MAY

5. YOU DO NOT HAVE YOUR BULLS

The answers are:

1. VENDO BARCOS EM JANEIRO, EM MARÇO, EM ABRIL, EM JUNHO E EM JULHO

2. O MEU LEITE ESTÁ FRIO EM NOVEMBRO E EM DEZEMBRO

3. HÁ QUATRO DOMINGOS EM AGOSTO

4. COMO OS SEUS PATOS EM FEVEREIRO E AS SUAS VACAS EM MAIO

5. NÃO TEM OS SEUS TOUROS

A NOTE ON EUROPEAN AND BRAZILIAN PORTUGUESE

The difference between the Portuguese spoken in Portugal and that of Brazil is something like the difference between British and American English – but if anything a little more marked.

There are a few differences of pronunciation, but in fact it is easier for a British person learning Portuguese to understand the language spoken in Brazil, since the vowels are not "swallowed" as much as in Portugal (and, therefore, as they are on the audio tape). Also, Brazilians tend to talk more slowly.

There are some small differences in the grammar of the two versions of the language, and some words which have different meanings. They don't affect either speaking or understanding all that much. Nevertheless, some of the European words in this course are not used in Brazil – so here is a list of the most important ones:

English	Portuguese	Brazilian	Pronunciation
goodbye	adeus	até logo	(ATAY LOGOO)
toilet	casa de banho	banheiro	(BANYEROO)
bus	autocarro	ônibus	(ONEEBOOS)
train	comboio	trem	(TRAENG)
girl	rapariga	moça	(MOSA)
tobacco	tabaco	fumo	(FOOMOO)
grass	relva	grama	(GRAMA)
stamp	selo	estampilha	(ESTAMPEELYA)
lift	elevador	ascensor	(ASENSOR)

This is the end of the course. We hope you have enjoyed it! Of course words and grammar will not be remembered for ever without revision, but if you look at the book from time to time, you will be surprised at how quickly everything comes back.

When you go abroad, do not be too shy to try out what you have learnt. Your host will appreciate your making the effort to speak, even if you make mistakes. And the more you attempt to speak the more you will learn!

GLOSSARY

accident	acidente	breast	seio
address	direcção (f)	bridge	ponte (f)
already	já	brother	irmão
always	sempre	brown	castanho
ambulance	ambulância	brush	escova
anchovy	anchova	bucket	balde
ankle	tornozelo	building	edifício
apple	maçã	bull	touro
asparagus	espargo	bullfight	tourada
baby	bebé	bus	autocarro
bag	saco	business	negócio
bakery	padaria	butcher's shop	talho
balcony	varanda	butter	manteiga
bank	banco	button	botão
bath	banho	buys (or you	
bathroom	casa de banho	buy)	compra
	(f)	cake	bolo
battery	bateria	can (tin)	lata
beach	praia	car	carro
bed	cama	cashier	caixa (m or f)
belt	cinto	castle	castelo
between	entre	cat	gato
big	grande	cathedral	catedral (f)
bill	conta	chair	cadeira
bird	pássaro	cheap	barato
black	petro or negro	chemist's shop	farmácia
blanket	manta	cheque	cheque
blood	sangue	chicken	frango
blouse	blusa	cinema	cinema (m)
blue	azul	city	cidade (f)
boarding		clean	limpo
house	pensão (f)	clock	relógio
boat	barco	closed	fechado
bone	osso	coat	sobretudo
book	livro	coffee	café
boot (car)	mala	cold	frio
bottle	garrafa	comb	pente
boy	rapaz	concert	concerto
brand	marca	convenient	conveniente
bread	pão	cool	fresco
breakdown	avaria	cork	rolha
breakfast	pequeno-almoço	cough	tosse (f)

cow	vaca	fig	figo
cup	chávena	finger	dedo
cupboard	armário	fire	fogo
curtain	cortina	first	primeiro
cushion	almofada	fish	peixe
customs	alfândega	floor	chão
dairy	leitaria	floor (storey)	andar
dance	dança	flower	flor (f)
dangerous	perigoso	fly	mosca
daughter	filha	food	comida
day	dia (m)	foot	pé
deckchair	cadeira de	forest	floresta
	repouso (f)	fork	garfo
dentist	dentista (m or	free	livre
	f)	fresh	fresco
department	departamento	frontier	fronteira
diet	dieta	fruit	fruta
difficult	difícil	garage	garagem (f)
dinner	jantar	garden	jardim
dirty	sujo	garlic	alho
disco	discoteca	gentlemen	senhores
doctor	médico	girl	rapariga
dog	cão	good	bom (boa)
door	porta	goodbye	adeus
drawer	gaveta	goose	ganso
dress	vestido	grape	uva
drink	bebida	grass	relva
driver	condutor	green	verde
duck	pato	half	meia
ear	ouvido	hand	mão (f)
easy	fácil	harbour	porto
eats	come	hard (not soft)	duro
egg	ovo	has	tem
elevator (lift)	elevador	hat	chapéu
embassy	embaixada	have (I)	tenho
empty	vazio	hello	olá
entrance	entrada	here	aqui
excellent	excelente	high	alto
excursion	excursão (f)	horse	cavalo
exhaust	tubo de escape	hospital	hospital
exit	saída	hot	quente
expensive	caro	hour	hora
eye	olho	house	casa
factory	fábrica	how	como
farm	quinta	how much	quanto
father	pai	husband	marido

ice cream	gelado	on	em
ill	doente	onion	cebola
in	em	open	aberto
insect	insecto	outside	fora de
insurance	seguro	owner	proprietário
jellyfish	alforreca	pain	dor (f)
job	emprego	palace	palácio
kitchen	cozinha	park	parque
knife	faca	party	festa
label	etiqueta	passport	passaporte
ladies	senhoras	path	caminho
lake	lago	pear	pera
last	último	pepper	pimenta
launderette	lavandaria	perfume	perfume
less	menos	petrol	gasolina
letter	carta	picnic	piquenique
lettuce	alface (f)	plant	planta
lobster	lagosta	plate	prato
manager	gerente	please	por favor
map	mapa (m)	police	policia
market	mercado	post office	correio
match	fósforo	potato	batata
mattress	colchão	prawn	gamba
meat	carne (f)	pump	bomba
menu	menú	puncture	furo
message	recado	purse	bolsa
midday	meio-dia (m)	quarter	quarto
midnight	meia-noite (f)	quick	rápido
milk	leite	quiet	tranquilo
minute	minuto	rabbit	coelho
mirror	espelho	radiator	radiador
money	dinheiro	rain	chuva
month	mês	receipt	recibo
morning	manhã	red	vermelho
mosquito	mosquito	restaurant	restaurante
mother	mãe	rice	arroz
mountain	montanha	river	rio
mouth	boca	rock	rocha
museum	museu	roof	tecto
napkin	guardanapo	room	quarto
newspaper	jornal	rope	corda
night	noite (f)	rug	tapete
no	não	salad	salada
octopus	polvo	salesman	vendedor
oil	óleo	salmon	salmão
old	velho	salt	sal

242

sand	areia	tunny	atum
sardine	sardinha	turkey	perú
scarf	cachecol	ugly	feio
sea	mar	under	debaixo de
second	segundo	vegetable	legume
see (I)	vejo	village	aldeia
sees	vê	walk (a)	passeio
sells (or you sell)	vende	wall	parede (f)
service	serviço	walnut	noz (f)
shelf	prateleira	wants	quer
shirt	camisa	wardrobe	guarda-roupa (m)
shop	loja	washbasin	lavatório
shower	duche	water	água
sister	irmã	waterfall	cascata
skirt	saia	wave	onda
small	pequeno	week	semana
snow	neve (f)	wheel	roda
son	filho	when	quando
soup	sopa	where	onde
spoon	colher (f)	white	branco
stamp	selo	who	quem
steering wheel	volante	why	porque
street	rua	wife	esposa
sun	sol	window	janela
supermarket	supermercado	wine	vinho
supper	ceia	wood (timber)	madeira
swimmer	banhista (m or f)	yacht	iate
		year	ano
table	mesa	yellow	amarelo
tap	torneira	yes	sim
tax	imposto		
taxi	táxi		
telephone	telefone	**Numbers**	
thank you	obrigado	zero	zero
there	ali	one	um
thunderstorm	tempestade (f)	two	dois (duas)
ticket	bilhete	three	três
time	tempo	four	quatro
tired	cansado	five	cinco
toilet	retrete (f)	six	seis
tomato	tomate	seven	sete
towel	toalha	eight	oito
train	comboio	nine	nove
tree	árvore (f)	ten	dez
trousers	calças	eleven	onze

twenty	vinte	Wednesday	quarta-feira
twenty-five	vinte e cinco	Thursday	quinta-feira
		Friday	sexta-feira
		Saturday	sábado
Days of the Week		Sunday	domingo
Monday	segunda-feira		
Tuesday	terça-feira		

LINKWORD ON COMPUTER

First Courses
*FRENCH *GERMAN *SPANISH *ITALIAN
*GREEK   *RUSSIAN *DUTCH   *PORTUGUESE

On IBM PC & COMPATIBLES, APPLE II Series, MACINTOSH
and COMMODORE 64

GCSE LEVEL FRENCH

An extensive vocabulary and grammar up to GCSE level standard,
ideal as a follow-up course to the book or first course programs or as
a revision or "brush-up" course for the rusty!

Available on IBM PC & Compatibles.

All courses available from

U.S.A.

ARTWORX INC.,
1844 PENFIELD ROAD,
PENFIELD,
NEW YORK.

TEL: (716) 385 6120

LINKWORD AUDIO TAPES

An audio tape is available as an extra learning aid to accompany
this book.

It allows you to hear and to practise the correct pronunciation for
all the words used on this course.

The tape is available by mail order using the order form at the back
of this book.

Other LINKWORD AUDIO TAPES:

0552 13225X French
0552 132268 German
0552 132276 Spanish
0552 132284 Italian
0552 139556 Greek

LINKWORD LANGUAGE SYSTEM BOOKS, AUDIO TAPES AND BOOK AND TAPE PACKS AVAILABLE FROM CORGI BOOKS

THE PRICES SHOWN BELOW WERE CORRECT AT THE TIME OF GOING TO PRESS. HOWEVER TRANSWORLD PUBLISHERS RESERVE THE RIGHT TO SHOW NEW RETAIL PRICES ON COVERS WHICH MAY DIFFER FROM THOSE PREVIOUSLY ADVERTISED IN THE TEXT OR ELSEWHERE.